BROTHER ROGER
OF TAIZÉ

MODERN SPIRITUAL MASTERS
Robert Ellsberg, Series Editor

Already published:

MODERN SPIRITUAL MASTERS SERIES

BROTHER ROGER OF TAIZÉ

Essential Writings

Selected with an Introduction by

MARCELLO FIDANZIO

ORBIS BOOKS

Maryknoll, New York 10545

Founded in 1970, Orbis Books endeavors to publish works that enlighten the mind, nourish the spirit, and challenge the conscience. The publishing arm of the Maryknoll Fathers and Brothers, Orbis seeks to explore the global dimensions of the Christian faith and mission, to invite dialogue with diverse cultures and religious traditions, and to serve the cause of reconciliation and peace. The books published reflect the views of their authors and do not represent the official position of the Maryknoll Society. To learn more about Maryknoll and Orbis Books, please visit our website at www.maryknoll.org.

Copyright © 2006 by Ateliers et Presses de Taizé.

Published by Orbis Books, Maryknoll, NY 10545-0308.

Queries regarding rights and permissions should be addressed to:
Orbis Books, P.O. Box 308, Maryknoll, NY 10545-0308.

Manufactured in the United States of America.

Library of Congress Cataloging-in-Publication Data
Roger, frère, 1915-
  [Selections. English. 2006]
  Essential writings / Brother Roger of Taizé ; selected with an introduction by Marcello Fidanzio.
      p. cm. – (Modern spiritual masters series)
  Includes bibliographical references (p.).
  ISBN-13: 978-1-57075-639-9 (pbk.)
  1. Christian life. 2. Spirituality. I. Fidanzio, Marcello. II. Title. III. Series.
BV4501.3.R645 2006
248 – dc22
                                                                    2005025703

Contents

Jesus, our hope, make us into humble people of the Gospel. We would so much like to understand that the best in us is built up by a very simple trust. . . . Even a child can manage it.

— *Brother Roger*

Preface

For many people, the name of Taizé evokes first of all a kind of music or a style of prayer. After all, the songs of the Taizé community, known for their simplicity and their contemplative quality, have spread far and wide from the village in France where they originated, and today they are sung by people of every church tradition on every continent. Others know Taizé as a place of pilgrimage that each year brings together countless young people from across the globe. For others still, Taizé signifies the existence of a small community, uniting brothers from different Christian denominations in a simple common life in the monastic tradition. All of this was rooted in the faith and vision of one man, Brother Roger, the founder and prior of the Taizé community.

For that reason, Christians across the world were shaken by the news that on the night of August 16, 2005, Brother Roger had been attacked and killed during evening prayers by a young woman, probably mentally disturbed, amid a congregation of twenty-five hundred young people. He was ninety years old.

The thousands of tributes that poured in over the following days bear witness to the love and respect in which Brother Roger was held. They came from church leaders of all denominations, heads of state, ordinary women and men of every nationality, and especially from young people, with whom he had enjoyed a special rapport.

Who then was Brother Roger?

9

Son of a Swiss pastor and a French mother, Brother Roger gave his entire life to the founding and leading of an ecumenical community that he hoped would be a small sign of reconciliation among Christians, a small leaven of peace and hope.

Situated in the tiny village of Taizé in the Burgundy region of France, not far from the ruins of the ancient monastery of Cluny, which had such great influence throughout the Middle Ages, the community now numbers about a hundred brothers, Catholics or from various Protestant backgrounds, representing over twenty nationalities. It is above all a place of prayer and of welcome. Since the 1960s, hundreds of thousands of young people have visited the community every year. They stay for a week of prayer, discussion, practical work, and searching together "at the sources of faith" for a meaning to their lives. When they return home, many of them profoundly touched by the experience, the community encourages them not to form any sort of movement, but to involve themselves in the life of their local churches, of whatever tradition, or to take on responsibilities to promote peace and reconciliation in their society.

The community has received many distinguished visitors, including Pope John Paul II, several archbishops of Canterbury, and Orthodox metropolitans. But its influence has been above all an extremely personal one, touching countless visitors in ways that will perhaps echo throughout their lives. A great part of this is due to the personality of the founder, to the clarity of his intuitions, to his capacity to communicate by a gesture, a short phrase, in silence, and on the level of the heart.

The English edition of this anthology was in preparation at the time of Brother Roger's death. Thus, it becomes something of a testament, in which the essentials of his vision are expressed in his own words. It is offered in the hope that, through his words, Brother Roger's vision will inspire new readers to take up that vision and to continue his journey on the road to peace.

Introduction

The Man

To introduce the figure of Brother Roger, it is appropriate to begin with the experience of his maternal grandmother. During the First World War she was a widow, living in the north of France not far from the battlefields. In spite of the bombings, she decided not to leave the zone where she lived, and she turned her home into a place of welcome for refugees. Brother Roger remembers well the evening when his grandmother came to his parents' home, after having been forced to flee her village when it was abandoned. As the youngest of his parents' nine children, he was the first to greet her. Shortly afterward his grandmother fainted; she had exhausted herself in welcoming others. Brother Roger also remembers how his grandmother suffered at seeing Christians, divided into different denominations, fighting and killing one another in Europe. "They at least should be reconciled, in order to avoid another war," she would often say. Although she belonged to a family that had been Protestant for generations, to live out reconciliation within herself she would sometimes go into a Catholic church to pray. Those two aspirations of his grandmother — welcoming those in need and seeking reconciliation among Christians — deeply marked the life of the future founder of Taizé.

When he was a teenager, Roger fell ill with tuberculosis. He remained an invalid for several years and at one point was even in danger of death. He was forced to interrupt his studies and to recuperate in the mountains, where he spent his time reading and taking long walks in the woods. "Those were years in which I was aware that I was building myself up within," he later recalled. "I began to realize that a God of love and compassion cannot be the author of suffering. And I made this discovery as well: it is not prestigious gifts or great talents that enable us to be creators in God. A great inspiration can be born even in times of trial. My illness prepared the future; God's call was in a certain sense linked to a difficulty, even if I was not yet able to understand how."

During his university years, Roger's searching was enriched by the discovery of new realities. Together with a few companions, he thought about the problem of isolation in living out one's faith, a problem that young people often have after they finish their studies. "How can we keep our own searching alive? How can we continue the good that has begun in us?" With them he discovered the need to go beyond a purely individual vision of faith, and he experienced the advantages of sharing and mutual support, to the point where the ideal of life in community opened up for him.

In 1940 Roger was twenty-five, and a new war was dividing Europe. At that time of great suffering, he decided to leave neutral Switzerland and to settle in Taizé, a small village in Burgundy near the line of demarcation that divided Vichy France from the area under Nazi occupation. His desire was to help those in difficulty as well as to create a base for an experience of community life. "The more a believer wishes to live the absolute call of God," he would write later, "the more he or she has to insert that absolute into human misery." He began to offer hospitality to political refugees, especially Jews. In 1942 he was forced to take refuge in Switzerland because of raids by the Nazis; three other young men came to join him there. Together they returned to Taizé in the autumn of 1944, and on Easter 1949 the first seven brothers committed themselves for life to material and spiritual sharing, to celibacy, and to a common life lived in great simplicity. Brother Roger became prior. He often used the expression "taking risks to proclaim the @@Gospel": these words must be lived out each day in a new and different way according to the possibilities of each person and the circumstances in which they find themselves.

In the life of Brother Roger and in the growth of the Taizé community, a critical moment came in 1958 at a meeting with Pope John XXIII. Through him the brothers of Taizé realized that to live an authentic reconciliation among Christians, it was necessary to highlight the ministry of the bishop of Rome as universal pastor and to discover a communion with him. Through the intervention of Cardinal Pierre-Marie Gerlier, then archbishop of Lyons, Brother Roger was received by the newly consecrated Pope John XXIII on his first day of audiences. "The pope showed great interest in our life," said the founder of Taizé. "When we spoke of reconciliation, he clapped his hands and exclaimed: Bravo! He was an open man, full of joy and spontaneity." Beginning with that first meeting, a strong link was established between the two men, nourished by mutual affection. Brother Roger had an audience with the pope each year and this tradition continued with his successors. Pope John had a profound influence on the community's ongoing life. But the influence was perhaps mutual. In 1960, seeing Brother Roger arrive, the pope greeted him with words that have become famous: "Ah, Taizé, that little springtime!"

Brother Roger was a man who listened. For many years, every evening he remained in the church at the end of the prayers to meet with those who wished to speak with him. Together with his brothers, he said he did not wish to be a spiritual master for the young, but rather to set out with them on the road to Christ. What was striking was the attentiveness with which he listened to the person in front of him: the passing of time or the number of other people waiting seemed not to have any importance; his attention was always fixed on the person with whom he was speaking. To lead to Christ and to reawaken hope, he used very simple means: not just words, but also silences, exclamations of wonder, a prayer recited together. And also looks, expressions, the sign of the cross made on the forehead of those who could not find words to communicate. A few years ago Cardinal Carlo Maria Martini, the archbishop of Milan, said that with his eyes and his gestures Brother Roger demonstrated the new life that is the fruit of baptism. These gifts were not taken for granted by the founder of Taizé; he forced himself to give as much as he could in order to communicate them to those he met.

When you spoke with Brother Roger, you really had the feeling that you were walking together on the same road. In addition to supporting those he met, he also let himself be encouraged by younger people and was visibly consoled by them. Sometimes at the end of a conversation he would say, "It was an exchange," meaning that there was a true reciprocity. Despite his long life, he never stopped searching.

The Writings

The writings of Brother Roger span a very long period of time, from 1941 to his death in 2005, and they are linked to his commitment to the Taizé community. When he was young, Roger Schutz-Marsauche wanted to be a writer, and to prepare himself for this he planned to study literature. He even wrote an autobiographical essay entitled *Evolution of a*

Puritan Youth and went to Paris to present it to the *Nouvelle Revue Française,* which in those days was very well known. The editor intended to publish it, but asked him to modify the conclusion. Roger felt he could not do this and so chose to give up all thought of a career as a writer. Wishing to express the radical nature of his decision, he burned the manuscript of the essay and followed the intuition that led him, after studying theology, to begin the experience of community life. In fact, later on, he wrote a lot, but always in a functional way linked to the needs of his ministry within the community and the activities in which the Taizé brothers were involved.

It is not hard to distinguish different phases in the writings of Brother Roger, because in successive periods he dealt with different topics using different literary genres. In the first period, beginning in 1941, he wrote on community life for the purpose of making his project known and then of structuring the Taizé community that was coming into being. Brother Roger prepared books of modest dimensions, often composed of short texts that communicated in a simple and direct fashion. This would remain a constant of his way of writing: not to say more than necessary, but in a few lines to go to the heart — the essential, as he liked to say — of what he wished to communicate. The most significant of these texts are *The Rule of Taizé* (1953) and *Unanimity in Pluralism* (1966), written in continuity with the rule. *The Rule of Taizé* is perhaps the best known of Brother Roger's writings, at least when all the various editions published in many languages are taken into account. It was born of the desire of the first brothers to have a point of reference to which they could always return. It is not a juridical document but wishes rather to set down "the essential aspects that make a common life possible." The rule is very much in harmony with the texts of the Church Fathers, St. Benedict in particular. (Interestingly, Brother Roger's thesis for his theology degree dealt with the early monastic rules leading up to that of St. Benedict.)

At around the same time, Brother Roger wrote three small books about Christian witness in the contemporary world and about ecumenism: *Living Today for God* (1958), *Unity: Man's Tomorrow* (1962), and *The Dynamic of the Provisional* (1965). These topics were close to his heart and still today are a key part of the community's outlook.

Beginning in the early 1960s, young adults in ever increasing numbers came to Taizé to share the prayer of the community, to meet together, and to be listened to by the brothers. Particularly after the upheavals of 1968, many came to Taizé with burning questions and often with their hearts marked by deep disappointments. The community and its founder strove above all to listen to the young, to help them to rediscover hope, and to invite them to commit themselves to the renewal of the Church. The writings of Brother Roger changed along with this: before the events of May 1968 in France he had prepared a new book, but a number of encounters that took place after that date caused him to rewrite it. Together with his reflections, he added many pages from his personal journal in which he recounted what he had heard and the replies he was able to give. With *Violent for Peace* (1968) a new period began in the writings of the founder of Taizé: for many years following, he would publish excerpts from his personal journal in which he shared with the readers the experiences, intuitions, and sensations that filled his days. These works contain many poetic passages that show his contemplative way of looking at what surrounded him. The titles chosen for these books recapitulate the best of what he discovered and lived out in those years: *Festival* (1971), *Struggle and Contemplation* (1973), *A Life We Never Dared Hope For* (1976), *The Wonder of a Love* (1979), *And Your Deserts Shall Flower* (1982), *A Heart That Trusts* (1985).

To support the searching of the young, from 1980 on, the Taizé community began a "pilgrimage of trust on earth." This pilgrimage does not organize young people into a movement, but stimulates them to be promoters of peace and bearers of trust and reconciliation in the places where they live. To accompany the different stages of this pilgrimage of trust, each year Brother Roger would write a letter that formed the starting point for the reflection during the meetings organized by the community. The letter was translated into some sixty different languages and was often written while Brother Roger spent time in a place of poverty and division, sharing the life of those undergoing trials. Before his death, Brother Roger had written thirty such letters, beginning with *Living beyond Every Hope* (1974) up to *A Future of Peace* (2005).

In 1990, to mark the fiftieth anniversary of Taizé, Brother Roger significantly revised the text of the community's rule and proposed a new formulation that attempted to express only what was most essential. For several years he had decided to abandon the expression "rule," which he considered too legalistic, and to speak instead of the "sources of Taizé." The text was published with the title *No Greater Love: The Sources of Taizé*. Even then Brother Roger continued to work on the text, and a new edition was published in 2001. In his later years he came out with two other little books, a fruit of this work of revision of his previous writings to which he constantly dedicated himself: *Peace of Heart in All Things* (1995), in which he offered short meditations for every day of the year, and *God Is Love Alone* (2001), which, as the blurb says, "brings together the key topics of his reflection as well as accounts of events or encounters that have marked his life, often very personal ones."

In addition to his own writings, Brother Roger wrote three books with Mother Teresa of Calcutta as a result of their great inner accord and collaboration: *Meditation on the Way of the Cross* (1986); *Mary, Mother of Reconciliation* (1987); *Prayer: Seeking the Heart of God* (1992).

Speaking of the writings of the founder of Taizé, the Orthodox theologian Olivier Clément told of his own experience: "I was deeply moved by the brief and luminous texts of Brother Roger, some of which are collected in volumes that you would like to carry about with you, maybe like carrying a gourd of fresh water in the desert."

The Message

"Love, and say it with your life," said St. Augustine. Without a love that forgives, without reconciliation, what future is possible for human beings? At the beginning of the new millennium, in some people there is an impulse to seek reconciliation, not just among Christians, but in the most diverse situations among peoples, in families as well as with nonbelievers. An ecumenical vocation that is not made concrete in reconciliation becomes something illusory.

When the founder of Taizé was asked what he wanted to express with his life, he often replied by recalling what his grandmother did before him: "Her witness opened a very concrete path for me. Her commitment to welcome the poor and to seek reconciliation in the depths of her being marked me for life. I found my identity as a Christian by reconciling within myself the faith of my origins with the mystery of the Catholic faith, without breaking communion with anyone." In founding the Taizé community, Brother Roger tried to open up new roads to heal the divisions that tear Christians apart and, through their reconciliation, to find ways beyond conflicts in the human family.

To be reconciled and to commit oneself to alleviate the sufferings of the weakest are realities to which Brother Roger had dedicated himself since he was young. For the founder of Taizé, the wellspring from which this kind of commitment can spring is found in the search for a life of communion with God. He devoted himself constantly to transmitting this reality, as much in the words he spoke as in the acts that filled his days. His conviction was that, today more than ever, Christian witness consists in committing oneself to make one's own life a reflection of the Gospel as clearly and transparently as possible.

Brother Roger spoke of the relationship with God as something that is present in the depths of every human being: "Communion with the living God touches what is unique and most intimate in the depths of the being." Sometimes God's presence is more evident; other times it is more hidden. Inspired by St. Augustine, he presented a very simple path whereby each person can discover the possibility to live in communion with God: "The simple desire for God is already the beginning of faith."

At the heart of his searching, Brother Roger discovered God's love for each person. Some words from the Gospel of John were particularly dear to him and he often called them to mind, reformulating them in this way: "Jesus, the Christ, did not come to earth to judge the world, but so that through him every human being might be saved, reconciled."

The founder of Taizé considered that one of the greatest obstacles to faith is the idea that God torments and condemns
human beings. So on every occasion possible he spoke about
a God who loves and forgives: "God loves us.... All God
can do is love." Similar expressions repeated dozens of times
in his writings are the best synthesis of what Brother Roger
communicated to those around him.

When we discover how great God's forgiveness is, we are
impelled more and more strongly to forgive one another. The
Rule of Taizé recalls this phrase that Brother Roger's mother
often used to repeat: "If we were to lose mercy, we would
have lost everything." A life of communion with God opens
us to seek reconciliation with others and to commit ourselves
to alleviate the sufferings of the poorest.

Roger often confessed his own fears and difficulties without embarrassment. He loved to receive questions, but he
did not feel obliged to have an answer for everything: sometimes he could only remain in silence or admit his concern;
when things came up where he had made discoveries, however, he would be extremely animated in explaining the point
he had reached. When you met him, you realized that each
day, in order to find his own road, he must have taken into
account the same difficulties as those who come to the hill
of Taizé, and that his own searching took place within these
difficulties. Thus for each person it was perhaps possible to
begin a similar journey: to open up to hope, to run the risk
of trusting, to seek peace of heart, to do everything so that
joy can remain. The realities of which he spoke were not ac-
quired once and for all, but had continually to be sought
and rediscovered. Speaking about Taizé and about all that
had come about, beginning from his own commitment, he
explained that "we can build only by starting from what we

are, with our limits and our frailties. God places a treasure of the Gospel in the vessels of clay that we are."

"Maybe the secret," wrote Hubert Beuve-Méry, the publisher of the newspaper *Le Monde,* after a visit to Taizé in 1957, "already lies in the naked hands of seemingly destitute men who are seeking to reconstruct a scale of values and to rediscover a style of life. Perhaps what is missing most in this world, a prey to all kinds of vertigo, is only something similar to Cluny, with all the adaptations which the twentieth century requires."

Chronology

1915   Roger Louis Schutz-Marsauche is born on May 12, in the village of Provence in French-speaking Switzerland. He is the ninth child of Charles Schutz and his wife, Amélie Marsauche.

1918   Meets his mother's mother for the first time. Her witness will be of great importance for his life.

1931   Contracts tuberculosis. This illness lasts for several years. Due to a relapse, for a time he is in danger of death.

1936   Following his father's wishes, begins to study theology in Lausanne and Strasbourg.

1937   In his youth goes through a period of doubt. "I did not really call into question the existence of God," he would write later. "My doubts concerned communion with God, communication. I did not feel I could honestly pray." During the summer of 1937, when one of his sisters was ill, he found he could say Psalm 27: "I am seeking your face, O Lord." Several months later he rediscovers trust by reading in an old book that "Christ is the one who enables us to know God."

1939   Chosen as president of the Christian Student Fellowship. The meetings he organizes are very popular and lead to the formation of a group that meets regularly for dialogue and retreats.

1940   Chooses to leave neutral Switzerland and go to
            France, which is divided in half by the advance of
            the German troops. In his heart there is the desire
            to bring a community into being. On August 20
            he discovers the village of Taizé, in Burgundy,
            close to the line of demarcation. He buys an old
            house and begins to offer hospitality to political
            refugees, mainly Jews.

1942   His activity is discovered by the police of the
            occupation. Warned just in time, he has to
            leave Taizé. For two years he lives in Geneva,
            Switzerland, with the first three brothers who
            join him. They return to Taizé in 1944.

1949   Seven brothers make a life commitment to a
            common life lived in great simplicity. Brother
            Roger is prior.
                That same year, at the suggestion of Cardinal
            Gerlier of Lyons, he goes to Rome for the first
            time and has an audience with Pope Pius XII.

1951   Now that there are twelve brothers, some are sent
            to share the life of the poorest in different parts
            of the world. Later Brother Roger will spend a
            few weeks each year in a place of poverty or
            division outside Europe; he will be in Chile after
            the coup d'état, in Lebanon during the war there,
            in South Africa, Calcutta....

1953   At Easter he presents the "Rule of Taizé," in
            which he indicates the essential aspects of the life
            of the growing community. Later on, the text will
            be known as the *Sources of Taizé.*

1958   First meeting with John XXIII. Pope John will
        be a point of reference for the community.
        Beginning with this meeting, Brother Roger will
        have audiences with the popes at least once
        a year.

1961   Brother Roger invites Catholic bishops and
        Protestant ministers to Taizé for three days. It
        is one of the first meetings of this sort since the
        Reformation in the sixteenth century.

1962   Visit to Constantinople to see the Orthodox
        Patriarch Athenagoras, with whom he will meet
        on several occasions. On the way back, first visit
        to Eastern Europe (Bulgaria and Yugoslavia);
        later on he will return there several times (Poland,
        East Germany, Hungary, Czechoslovakia, Russia,
        Romania) until the fall of the Berlin Wall.
            That same year, Brother Roger is invited to
        participate in the Second Vatican Council as an
        observer. Together with Brother Max, he will
        take part in all the sessions of the Council until
        its closing in 1965.

1963   Takes part in the millennium celebrations of
        Mount Athos.

1966   First international meeting of young adults
        organized in Taizé. For several years, young
        people had been coming to Taizé spontaneously
        in ever growing numbers.

1974   Goes to London to receive the Templeton Prize
        for the progress of religion; in Frankfurt receives
        the German Peace Prize. Opening a "Council of
        Youth" in Taizé, he writes his first letter, and

from then on writes an open letter to the young each year.

1976   Mother Teresa of Calcutta makes her first visit to Taizé; in the same year he goes to Calcutta together with some brothers.

1978   Accompanied by children from every continent, brings to the Secretary General of the United Nations, Javier Pérez de Cuellar, the suggestions of the young on how the UN can create trust between peoples. The same year, goes to Madras (India) for the first intercontinental meeting prepared by the Taizé community in the southern hemisphere.

1986   Pope John Paul II visits Taizé.

1988   Takes part in Moscow in the celebrations for the millennium of Christianity in Russia. The same year, receives the UNESCO prize for peace education.

1989   In Germany receives the international Karlspreis: "The balance which Taizé tries to find," explains the jury, "can be a model to end the tensions in Europe, not only on the religious level, but also on the political one." At the end of the year goes to Poland for the first young adult European meeting organized by the Taizé community in Eastern Europe.

1992   The archbishop of Canterbury, Dr. George Carey, spends a week in Taizé in the company of a thousand young Anglicans. The same year, in Strasbourg, Brother Roger receives the Robert

Schuman Award for his contribution to the building up of Europe.

1995   Goes to Johannesburg, South Africa, for an international meeting of young Africans organized by the Taizé community.

1997   Is invited to speak at the ecumenical assembly in Graz.

2004   Goes to Lisbon for the twenty-seventh young adult European meeting prepared by the Taizé community.

2005   On August 16, during a prayer service at Taizé, Brother Roger is fatally wounded by a mentally unbalanced assailant. He dies at the age of ninety.

1

A Parable of Community

A Community of Kindness of Heart and Simplicity

When I was still a child, some summer afternoons we would get together to read texts aloud. Among the stories that were often read were some excerpts of the history of Port-Royal, written by Sainte-Beuve. It told of a Cistercian community of women that lived near Paris in the seventeenth century.

When the abbess died in 1602, Angélique Arnauld, the daughter of a Parisian lawyer, replaced her. According to the custom of the time, her grandfather had taken steps to ensure that she would be elevated to that office despite her young age. She remained in the monastery against her wishes and lived there for several years in great inner distress.

One day, writes Sainte-Beuve, when the young abbess was seventeen years old, a priest passed through and gave a meditation to the community. It was common knowledge that this priest led a disordered life, but that day he expressed clearly God's love, his inexhaustible and unlimited goodness. Those words caused an inner upheaval in the young Angélique Arnauld: "God touched me so deeply that, from that moment on, I considered myself more fortunate to be a religious than I had previously thought myself unfortunate to be one."

As a result, returning to the wellsprings of their vocation, she introduced radical changes in the life of the community; gradually it became known far and wide and had a great impact. Among others, Blaise Pascal's sister entered the community. Men came to live beside the monastery for shorter or longer periods of prayer and study; they were known as the "Messieurs de Port-Royal."

My mother had so much admiration for that period of the history of Port-Royal-des-Champs that she had placed a portrait of Mother Angélique Arnauld on her desk. "She's my invisible friend," she used to say.

And myself, I was captivated to discover what a few women, living in community, had been able to accomplish. Close to our house there was a large yew tree with very dense foliage. One day when I was about sixteen, I stopped by that tree and said to myself, "If those few women, responding in all lucidity to a call to community life and giving their life for Christ, had so much impact on those around them, could not a few men living in community do the same thing?"

Since then, I think that I never lost the intuition that community life could be a sign that God is love, and love alone. Gradually the conviction took shape in me that it was essential to create a community with men determined to give their whole life and who would always try to understand one another and be reconciled, a community where kindness of heart and simplicity would be at the center of everything.

— *God Is Love Alone*, 22–24

You Are No Longer Alone

Desiring as you do to give your life because of Christ and the Gospel (Mk 10:29, Mt 16:25) always keep in mind that you are advancing with him toward the light, even in the midst of your own darkness.

So, no longer looking back (Lk 9:62), run forward in the footsteps of Jesus the Christ. He is leading you along a path of light: I am, but also, you are the light of the world (Jn 8:12, Mt 5:14).

You wish to prepare the ways of the Lord Christ for many others (Mk 1:3), kindling a fire even in the world's darkest nights (Lk 12:49).

You know that Jesus the Christ came for all (Titus 2:11), not just for a few. Risen, he is united with every human being without exception. Such is the catholicity of heart God has set within you.

Will you let an inner life grow within you, one which has neither beginning nor end? There, you stand at the threshold of the Gospel's joy, where human solidarities plunge their roots.

Making the earth a place where all can live, be they nearby or far away, is one of the beautiful pages of the Gospel for you to write by your life.

By forgetting yourself, by not seeking your own advantage, you are enabled to stand firm in the midst of the human family's situations with all their constant ebb and flow. Will you seek to understand, without letting yourself be carried away by the successive waves?

By sharing, are you among those who, with very little, generate a fine human hope?

With almost nothing, are you a creator of reconciliation in that communion of love which is the Body of Christ, his Church?

Sustained by a shared momentum, rejoice. You are no longer alone; in all things you are advancing together with your brothers. With them, you are called to live the parable of community.   — *The Sources of Taizé*, 48–49

Peace of Heart

The peace of your heart makes life beautiful for those around you.

Being wracked with worry has never been a way of living the Gospel. Founding your faith on torment would mean building a house on sand (Mt 7:26–27).

At every moment, do you hear these words of Jesus the Christ: "Peace I leave you; my peace I give you. Let your hearts cease to be troubled and afraid" (Jn 14:27)?

This deep-seated peace provides the lightness needed to set out once again, when failure or discouragements weigh on your shoulders.

And sheer wonder comes alive, along with a breath of poetry, a simplicity of life and, for those able to understand it, a mystical vision of the human person.

For you this Gospel prayer: *Bless us, Lord Christ; bless us and those you have entrusted to us. Keep us in the spirit of the Beatitudes* (Mt 5:3–12), *joy, simplicity, mercy.*

Joy. Peace of heart is a mainstay of the inner life; it sustains us as we make our way upward toward joy.

Peace and joy are Gospel pearls. They come to fill chasms of anxiety.

Will you welcome each new day as God's today? In every season, will you find ways of discovering life's poetry, on days full of light as in winter's frozen nights? Will you discover how to bring joy to your humble dwelling by small signs that cheer the heart?

The presence of the Risen Christ leads to unexpected moments of happiness; it breaks through your nights. "Darkness is not darkness with you; the night shines bright as day" (Ps 139:12).

Do not be afraid of suffering. In the very depths of the abyss, a perfection of joy can be found in communion with Christ Jesus.

Dare to rejoice in what God is accomplishing through you and around you. Then all forms of pessimism about yourself and about others, which were waging war on your soul, will melt away.

If you forgot the gifts of the Holy Spirit (2 Tim 1:6–7) in you, and if you lost the last traces of self-esteem, then what a risk of losing your balance...! The void attracts, fascinates.

With joy comes a sense of wonder. Such a joy needs nothing less than our whole being in order to shine forth. It lies in the transparent openness of peaceful love.

Unless the grain of wheat dies...(Jn 12:24). Paschal joy, the joy of Easter, brings healing to the secret wounds of the soul. It does not make the heart proud. It can do without applause. It goes straight to the gateways of light.

Simplicity. Through the Gospel, you have heard of the young man searching in God for the will of his love. He came to Christ with his questioning. One day Jesus addressed this call to him. It is one of the most astonishing in the Gospel: "There is one thing you lack: sell what you have, give the money to the poor, then come, follow me" (Mt 19:21). And the young man went away sad.

Why did he go away? Because he had great possessions. He wanted to follow Christ and at the same time hold on to his riches. He did not have the freedom to give, through love, even what he possessed.

Our vocation as community has committed us to live solely from our work, accepting neither donations nor bequests nor gifts — nothing, absolutely nothing.

The boldness involved in not ensuring any capital for ourselves, without fear of possible poverty, is a source of incalculable strength.

The spirit of poverty does not consist in looking poverty-stricken, but in arranging everything with imagination, in creation's simple beauty.

Happy all who love simplicity: in them is the Kingdom of God (Mt 5:3).

A constant simplifying of our existence keeps us far from those tortuous paths where we go astray.

Simplicity devoid of burning charity is a shadow without light. If a great simplicity of life were full of bitterness and laden with judgments, then where would be the joyfulness of each present day?

Sunlight breaking suddenly through the clouds: when the energies of the prime of life combine in you with the spirit of childhood, your soul draws near to serene joy.

Mercy. If you were to lose mercy, heartfelt compassion, you would have lost everything.

Will you let yourself be challenged by that absolute of love, the call to forgive even seventy times seven times, in other words always? (Mt 18:21–22).

With lightened step, you will go forward from one discovery to another.

For those who love and forget themselves, life is filled with serene beauty. All friendship involves an inner struggle. And sometimes the cross comes to illuminate the unfathomable depth of loving.

Rather than trying to impose yourself by creating a bad conscience around you, or slipping into an ironic tone, will you let yourself overflow with kindness?

In the transparency of this loving, admit your mistakes simply and do not waste time looking at the speck in your brother's eye (Mt 7:3–5).

Happy the community that becomes an abyss of kindness: it lets Christ shine through, incomparably.

Trust Is at Hand. Christ, love of all loving, is a fire that burns within you. And when love is forgiveness, your heart, though tested, begins to live once more.

The contemplation of his forgiveness becomes a radiant kindness in hearts that are simple. And the holiness of Christ is no longer out of reach.

We know him so little, but he is in our midst (Jn 1:26). And there arises a breath that will never die away . . . and that little is enough for us.

Do not be afraid, trust is at hand, and with it a happiness.
— *The Sources of Taizé,* 62–68

A First Rule of Life

While I was still young I had realized that I would need a point of reference on which to build, references taken from the Gospels which spoke powerfully to me. Without something very central to which I would return throughout my life, how would I ever develop myself within? It was not that I wanted to make some sort of system, but that I hoped to create a little inner unity. If it was going to be a question of taking great risks for God and for Christ — and it was risks and not ease I hoped for — there would be a need to keep a watch on myself, to refer to something which throughout my life would be a point of reference, something constantly to return to.

— Throughout your day, let work and rest be quickened by the Word of God.

— Keep inner silence in all things so as to dwell with Christ.

— Be filled with the spirit of the Beatitudes, joy, simplicity, mercy.
    — Quoted by Kathryn Spink, *A Universal Heart*, 45ff.

The Life Commitment

Beloved brother, what are you asking for?
    The mercy of God and the community of my brothers.
May God complete in you what he has begun.
    Brother, you trust in God's mercy: remember that the Lord Christ comes to help the weakness of your faith; committing himself with you, he fulfils for you his promise:
    Truly, there is no one who has left everything because of Christ and the Gospel who will not receive a hundred times as much at present — brothers and sisters and mothers and children — and persecutions too, and in the age to come eternal life (Mk 10:29–30, Lk 18:29–30).
    This is a way contrary to all human reason; you can only advance along it by faith, not by sight (2 Cor 5:7), always

sure that whoever gives their life for Christ's sake will find it (Mt 16:25).

From now on walk in the steps of Christ. Do not be anxious about tomorrow (Mt 6:34). First seek God's Kingdom and its justice (Mt 6:33). Surrender yourself, give yourself, and good measure, pressed down, shaken together, brimming over, will be poured out for you.

Whether you wake or sleep, night and day the desire for trust in God and in your brothers springs up and grows, you do not know how (Mk 4:27).

Avoid making sure you are noticed by others to gain their admiration (Mt 6:31). Never let your inner life make you look sad, like a hypocrite who puts on a grief-stricken air to attract attention. Anoint your head and wash your face, so that only your Father who is in secret knows what your heart intends (Mt 6:16–18).

Stay simple and full of joy, the joy of the merciful, the joy of brotherly love.

Be vigilant. If you have to rebuke a brother, keep it between the two of you (Mt 18:15).

Be concerned to establish communion with your neighbor.

Be open about yourself, remembering that you have a brother whose charge it is to listen to you. Bring him your understanding so that he can fulfil his ministry with joy (Heb 13:17).

The Lord Christ, in his compassion and his love for you, has chosen you to be in the Church a sign of brotherly love. It is his will that with your brothers you live the parable of community.

So, refusing to look back (Phil 3:13), praising, blessing, and singing Christ your Lord.

Receive me, Lord Christ, and I will live; may my expectation be a source of joy.

Brother, remember that it is Christ who calls you and that it is to him that you are now going to respond.

Will you, for love of Christ, consecrate yourself to him with all your being?

I will.

Will you henceforth fulfil your service of God within our community, in communion with your brothers?

I will.

Will you, renouncing all ownership, live with your brothers not only in community of material goods but also in community of spiritual goods, in utter openness of heart?

I will.

Will you, in order to be more available to serve with your brothers, and in order to give yourself in undivided love to Christ, remain in celibacy?

I will.

Will you, so that we may be of one heart and one mind and so that the unity of our common service may be fully achieved, adopt the orientations of the community expressed by the prior, bearing in mind that he is a poor servant within the community?

I will.

Will you, always discerning Christ in your brothers, watch over them in good days and bad, in suffering and in joy?

I will.

In consequence, because of Christ and the Gospel, you are henceforth a brother of our community.

— *The Sources of Taizé,* 72–74

2

Listening with the Heart

A Healing of the Heart

By forgiving us, God buries our past in the heart of Christ and brings relief to the secret wounds of our being.

When we can express to God all that burdens our life and keeps us trapped beneath the weight of a judgment, then light is shed on the shadows within us. Knowing that we are listened to, understood, and forgiven by God is one of the sources of peace ... and our heart begins to find healing.

— *Peace of Heart in All Things, 57–58*

People Who Listen

For some forty years now, my brothers and I have been astonished to see young people coming to Taizé in ever greater numbers.

Seeing so many young faces on our hill, not only from Western and Eastern Europe, but also more and more from other continents, we realize that they come with vital questions, especially this one: how can I find a meaning for my life? Some of them ask: how is God calling me?

With those we welcome either in Taizé itself, or in the small communities where a few of our brothers live among the poorest in different parts of the world, or else during the meetings held in large cities, we want to look for ways of finding new vitality, of living Christ for others.

We want to be for them people who listen, never spiritual masters. To listen to them so that they can express not only their limits, their wounds, but also discover their gifts, and especially glimpse a life of communion with God, with Christ, with the Holy Spirit. — *God Is Love Alone*, 10–11

A Very Simple Trust

Are there realities which make life beautiful and of which it can be said that they bring a kind of fulfillment, an inner joy? Yes, there are. And one of these realities bears the name of trust.

Do we realize that what is best in each of us is built up through a simple trusting? This is something even a child can do.

But at every age, some people are marked by suffering — being abandoned by others, seeing those they love die. And for many people today the future is so uncertain that they lose all delight in life.

For all, the source of confident trust is in God. God is love (1 Jn 4:8) and forgiveness, and dwells at the center of each person's soul.

Trust does not make us forget the suffering of so many unfortunate people across the earth. Their trials make us reflect: how can we be people who, sustained by a life of communion in God, search with others for ways of making the earth a better place to live?

Trust does not lead us to flee responsibilities, but rather to remain present in places where human societies are in turmoil. It enables us to keep going forward even in the face of failures. This trust makes us able to love with a selfless love.

Today, many young people across the earth are trying to heal divisions in the human family. Their confident trust can make life beautiful around them. Are they aware that, so often, a hope shines out in them?

— Letter 1999–2001, 1–2

The Risen Christ Sheds His Light into Our Nights

O living God, even in our inner nights, and although we do not yet see clearly, you send your Holy Spirit upon each one of us. Your Spirit transfigures our worries and our refusals into the ability to set out again and again, a thousand times if necessary, on the road along which we give our life to the very end. If we were to awaken, one fine morning, in technological societies, highly functional, but where an inner life had been extinguished....

Everyone is familiar with the vast possibilities of science and technology to alleviate hunger and relieve physical suffering. But are we aware that these powerful means alone are not enough to make the earth a place fit to live?

If we were to forget the trusting of faith and the intelligence of the heart, so vital for the building up of the human family....

At this period of history, we are all attentive to this question: are the younger generations losing a sense of the mystery of faith?

When faced with the realities of that unique communion which is the Church, many young people are not hostile but

rather absent, half-asleep. If the question of our own transfiguration concerns us so deeply, that is because we want at
all costs not to be paralyzed, frozen by certain trials of the
Church and of the human family.

So we remember that Christ did not come to create one
more religion, but to offer to all a communion in him,
that unique communion which is the Church. And he has
compassion on what some people have to go through.

As far as the Church in its ecumenical vocation is concerned, today the urgent challenge goes far beyond a new
stage in ecumenism. Will we let the critical hour go by which
calls for nothing less than a new birth of the ecumenical
vocation, a transfiguration?

For each one of us, a transfiguration of our depths! What
does that mean?

We do not ask God for ecstasies or wonders that are too
much for us. All that can only lead us "elsewhere."

St. Paul expresses the Gospel reality of transfiguration
with deep intuition. He writes, "When I am weak, then I am
made strong in God."

In the lives of all of us, some events cause us to understand
that it is not prestigious gifts or taking the easy way out that
infallibly enable us to be creators in God.

We would never want a child or a young person to lose
hope because they have been humiliated. But how many
times do we make this discovery: when our childhood or
youth were mistreated and may have undergone deep humiliations, the compassion of Christ was always present, even if
we were unaware of it. And Christ can bring out of these
trials a great boldness to create in God, to take the risks
of faith. Thus it comes about that, in our inner nights, the
risen Christ sheds his gentle light. In other words, the Gospel
can provoke a reversal and even an upheaval: we discover

that Christ passes through our weaknesses, our failures, our refusals, even our anguish, and we realize at the same time that he gives us something of his own face. In other words, he transfigures and changes the depths of our being. When we recognize our limits, our frailties, and our poverty, then in the Holy Spirit God enables us to set out again with new vitality.

And what allows us to discover this transfiguration? With our thorns themselves, God lights a fire that never goes out. He fills us with those Gospel realities that are so essential to build us up within — peace of heart, joy, simplicity, the spirit of mercy.

We know well that in us there can be worry, fear of suffering, in short everything that stresses our hearts. Among other things, there are those imperceptible worries whose causes and origin we are unaware of.

The Church, through listening, through the sacrament of reconciliation, has always had what was needed so that these negative impressions we have concerning ourselves do not cause us to lose our balance.

"The Church has always had what was needed. . . . " These words are not mine. A long time ago, when I was still young, I had a conversation with a psychoanalyst I knew; I had asked him if he could help some people that I would entrust to him. I was thinking particularly about some religious in crisis who sometimes came to see me in Taizé.

That psychoanalyst replied to me: I am well able to analyze a human being, but it is much more difficult to bring him or her back into inner unity; the Church, on the other hand, has always exercised a ministry of listening. The Church has many men and women, often elderly, who have the gift of listening, the charism of discernment. The Church also has priests; it has everything needed, so only send me people who are really ill.

I never saw that psychoanalyst again. Recently he wrote me that one day he would like to come to Taizé. I wanted him to come but I did not answer him right away, and in the meantime he died. I would have liked to have seen him again to express my gratefulness, because he had the capacity to recognize his limits and because he was so attentive to the ministry of the Church.

This ministry of listening is still quite necessary today, at a time when human beings are so broken. What is sad is that inner worries can uproot the trusting of faith in people and make them forget that, in prayer, God, Christ and the Holy Spirit intervene constantly in our lives.

When inner aggressions manage to uproot the trusting of faith, then some people ask themselves: if I no longer rely on the trusting of faith, have I become an atheist? No, never! It is not a question of atheism; they are gaps of unbelief, nothing more.

Christ places us before a choice. In our inner life, at a given moment there is no other way out than a response of freedom. This response is that of casting ourselves into God as into a deep pit. And then wonder arises. It is not an abyss of darkness, but a chasm radiant with the brightness of the Risen Lord, an abyss of compassion.

— *Nel mistero della trasfigurazione:*
Giornate di spiritualità ad Ars e Taizé
(Milan: Ancora, 1992), 89–93

Seeking to Understand the Whole Person

More often than ever before young people ask me, "What is the most beautiful thing in your life?" Without hesitating I reply: first of all the common prayer, and in it, the long periods of silence. Then, immediately after that, the most beautiful thing in my life is this: when I am talking with someone alone, to perceive the whole human being, marked by a tragedy or by being torn apart within, and at the same time by the irreplaceable gifts through which the life of God in that person is able to bring everything to fulfillment.

It is essential to try to comprehend the whole person, by means of a few words or attitudes rather than by lengthy attempts at explanation. It is not enough simply to share what assaults a person within. It is even more vital to search for that special gift of God, the pivot of their whole existence. Once this gift (or gifts) has been brought to light, roads forward lie open.

No dwelling on the knots, failures, and conflicting forces; thousands of reasons for them can always be found. Move on as quickly as possible to the essential: uncovering the unique gift, the talents entrusted to every human being, intended not to lie buried but to be brought to full life in God.

The most beautiful thing in my life? I could go on forever: those rare occasions when I suddenly find myself free to drop everything and go out...walking for hours and conversing in the streets of some great city...sharing a meal with guests round a table.... — *A Life We Never Dared Hope For,* 65

His Love Is a Fire

Every human being yearns to love and be loved. But the question remains: why are some people aware that they are loved while others are not?

When we are listened to, wounds from a recent or distant past find relief. This can be the beginning of a healing of the soul.

Listen in others to what makes them feel bad about themselves. Try to understand what lies beneath their hearts. And little by little, even in a ground ploughed up by trials, God's hope can be can sensed, or at least a fine human hope.

It happens that, when we accompany another person, the one who listens is led to the essential themselves, although the other may be unaware of it.

Listen and keep on listening. . . . Those who make use of their intuition throughout their lifetime become able to understand almost without words those who come with something to confide. Listening in this way can contribute to a very broad vision of human beings, inhabited by both fragility and radiance, by fullness and the void.

Some years ago I met with a young priest from Italy every day for a week. In him I saw close at hand Christ's holiness in a human being. At times I could not say anything but, "Dare to weep!" Once I even took a handkerchief from my pocket for him.

Weep, because it is not possible to bear alone, in stony silence, the struggle he had to wage.

Face to face with him, I could touch on what it can mean for a person to be abandoned. There exist people of silence who radiate communion.

As the days went by, the face of Christ appeared in that man so harrowed by his struggles. The depth of his gaze could conceal nothing of his successive ordeals. He brought me into the heart of one of the greatest mysteries — the gift of one's entire existence for love.

Before parting, after so many days of closeness, I knelt for him to give me his blessing.   — *God Is Love Alone*, 24–26

Avoiding Rigid Judgments

How vigilant we must be not to stick any labels on anyone's forehead! Using expressions like "anguish," "pride," "jealousy" is not without consequences. Human beings so easily run the risk of looking for reasons, imaginary or not, to justify such judgments. Having a rigid image of another person can paralyze the whole evolution of that person's personality.
— *Peace of Heart in All Things*, 31

Entrusting the Trials of Others to God

To be compassionate does not mean suffering what someone else suffers so that we despair and sink together into the same misfortune. Compassion leads us to entrust the other person's trial to God, even when we have no solution or response to offer. — *Joy Untold* (Letter, 1998), 12

Awaken Others to Christ by the Life You Lead

Filled with the Holy Spirit, century after century Christians have communicated to others the trust of faith.

Will you, for your part, be one of those who open up the ways of the Risen Christ (Mt 3:3)? Or will you hesitate and say, "Why do you ask me to prepare ways of the Gospel for others? Can't you see that I am quite helpless, like a child?"

Who can tell all that certain children communicate through gifts they are still unaware of (Lk 9:46–48)? Some of them awaken others to God by the trust they display, by unexpected words.

You awaken others to Christ above all by the life you lead. Words alone can easily make do with illusions. When a small-group discussion turns into mere chatter about God, the Holy Spirit, or communion with Christ, is there still anything creative about it?

You communicate the life of the Risen Christ through a profound personal unselfishness, by forgetting about yourself.

Instead of short-lived outbursts of enthusiasm, will you fashion for yourself a steadfast heart so as to be faithful to the end? (see Rev 2:9–10, Sir 2:2).

— *The Sources of Taizé*, 30

What You Never Dared Hope For

In each person there is a portion of solitude which no human intimacy can ever fill.

Yet you are never alone. Let yourself be plumbed to the depths (Rom 8:27) and you will see that, in your heart of hearts, in the place where no two people are alike, Christ is waiting for you. And what you never dared hope for springs to life.

Christ came "not to abolish but to fulfil" (Mt 5:17). When you listen, in the silence of your heart, you realize that, far from humiliating human beings, he comes to transfigure even what is most disturbing in you.

Does discovering who you are awaken a kind of inner unrest? But who is going to condemn you when Jesus is praying for you? (Rom 8:34). If you started accusing yourself of all that is in you, would your nights and days be long enough?

When trials arise within you or misunderstandings arrive from without, never forget that in the same wound where the pangs of anxiety are seething, creative forces are also being born. And a way opens up that leads from doubt toward trusting, from dryness to a creation.

— *The Sources of Taizé*, 11

Joy

Six centuries before the coming of Christ, God spoke these challenging words: "Forget what has gone before; do not dwell on the past. See, I am doing a new thing! Now it springs up; do you not perceive it?" (Is 43:18–19).

Yes, we are astonished by an unsuspected joy: the Holy Spirit wants to turn us into beings that are utterly transparent, like the sky on a spring day.

The Gospel bears within it such a radiant hope and such a call to joy that we would like to communicate them to people close at hand and far away, by going even to the point of giving ourselves.

Where is the source of hope and of joy? It is in God, who tirelessly seeks us out and finds in us the profound beauty of the human soul.   — *Astonished by Joy* (Letter, 2000), 4

3

At the Sources of Faith

The Simple Desire for God

Right at the depth of the human condition lies the longing for a presence, the silent desire for a communion.

Could a doubt come welling up? The desire for God does not vanish for all that. Four centuries after Christ, a believer wrote down his conviction: "If you desire to know God, you already have faith." What is important at the outset is not vast knowledge. Time will come when that will be of great value. But it is through the heart, in the depths of themselves, that human beings begin to grasp the mystery of faith. An inner life is developed step by step.

So it becomes clear that faith — trusting in God — is a very simple reality, so simple that everyone could receive it. It is like surging upward again and again, a thousand times, throughout our life and until our very last breath.

— *Taizé: Trust on Earth,* 6

Who Is Jesus Christ?

Who is he, this Christ Jesus of whom the Gospel speaks?

From before the beginning of the universe, from all eternity, Christ was in God (see Jn 1:1–2).

He came among human beings as a humble man.

If Jesus had not lived among us, God would be far away, and even unattainable. But in his life, Jesus allowed God to shine through as he is (see Jn 14:9).

And today, risen from the dead, Christ lives in each one of us by the Holy Spirit (see Jn 14:16–29).

— *God Is Love Alone,* 15

The One We Do Not Know Is in Our Midst

The One we do not know is in our midst. More accessible for some, more hidden for others...with astonishment each of us might hear him say, "Why be afraid? I, Jesus, am here; I am the Christ. I loved you first (1 Jn 4:10, 19),...in you I have set my joy."

You know well enough how fragile your response is. Confronted with the unconditional challenges of the Gospel, there are times when you feel unprepared.

One of the very first believers already said to Christ, "I believe; help my unbelief" (Mk 9:24).

Know once and for all that neither doubts nor the impression that God is silent ever take his Holy Spirit away from you.

What God is asking is for you to surrender yourself to Christ in the trust of faith and to welcome his love.

Even though you are pulled in different directions, you alone have to make the choice; no one can make it for you.

— *The Sources of Taizé,* 8

Prayer, Source of Love

A thinker from Romania, Dimitru Staniloae, who had been in prison for his beliefs, wrote: "I looked for God in the people of my village, then in books and in ideas. But that brought me neither peace nor love. One day, while reading the Church Fathers (texts by Christians of the first centuries), I discovered that it was possible to encounter God really, through prayer. I gradually realized that God was close to me, that he loved me, and that if I let myself be filled by his love, my heart opened to others. I realized that love was a communion, with God and with others."

— *Astonished by Joy* (Letter, 2000), 2

A Kind of Inner Voice

God does not require of us, in our praying, extraordinary feats or superhuman efforts. In Christian history, many believers have lived lives rooted in the wellsprings of faith through a prayer quite poor in words.

Do you feel at a loss when confronted with that reality of prayer which, at first, seems so far beyond you? That has been true since the beginning of the Church. The apostle Paul wrote, "We do not know how to pray...." And he added: "...but the Holy Spirit comes to help our weakness and prays within us." Your heart can scarcely imagine it, but his Spirit is constantly active within you.

You aspire to feel the presence of God and you have the impression that nothing is there. Seven hundred years ago, a Christian named Meister Eckhart wrote, "Turning to God ...does not mean thinking continually about God. It would be impossible for human nature to always have God in our minds, and anyway it would not be the best thing. Human beings cannot be satisfied with a God in the mind. For in that case, when we stopped thinking about God, God too would vanish. God is beyond human thought. And the reality of God never disappears."

A simple prayer, like a soft sighing, like a child's prayer, keeps us alert. Has not God revealed to those who are little, to Christ's poor, what the powerful of this world have so much trouble understanding?

—*Prayer: Seeking the Heart of God*, 37–38

Faith Is a Simple Reality

Faith is a simple reality, both for the most uneducated person who cannot even read or write as well as for the most cultivated one. The Russian writer Tolstoy recounts that one day, while taking a walk, he met a peasant, and they had a conversation. The peasant said to Tolstoy, "I live for God." In four words he expressed the depths of his soul. And Tolstoy said to himself, "I have so much knowledge and culture, and yet I am unable to speak like this peasant."

Trust in God is not conveyed by means of arguments which want to persuade at all costs and so end up causing anxiety, and even fear. It is first of all in the heart, in the depths of our being, that a Gospel call is received.

—*God Is Love Alone*, 18

Peace of Heart

It is not easy for human words to express to God what lies in the depths of our being. Some days we pray with almost nothing. Remaining close to Christ in utter simplicity is already praying. And silence is sometimes everything in prayer.

Will you be able to welcome the Risen Christ even in the dry and thirsty ground of your body and your spirit? And the tiny, even hidden, event of your waiting causes springs of living water to well up: goodness of heart, looking beyond

present difficulties, and also that inner harmony created by
the life of the Holy Spirit poured out in us.

Will you remain in the Risen Christ's presence, during
those long periods of silence when at first you seem to be
in a desert? This silence seems to be nothing at all. But there,
courageous decisions come to fruition.

When you pray, it can happen that you ask Christ, "What
do you expect of me?" The day will come when you realize
that he expects a lot. He expects you to be, for others, a
witness of the trusting of faith, a kind of reflection of his
presence.

Don't worry if you know so little about praying. Founder-
ing in worry has never been a Gospel path. "No one can add
a single day to their life by worrying about it.... I give you
my peace.... Do not let your heart be troubled and afraid."

Fears and anxieties are part of our human condition, im-
mersed as we are in societies that are wounded and shaken.
Every human being, every believer, journeys, creates, and
suffers in these societies, and can experience inner impulses
of revolt, sometimes of hatred and of domination.

By his Holy Spirit, the Risen Christ transfigures all that
is most disconcerting in you. He reaches what was out of
reach. All forms of pessimism that you harbor about yourself melt away; you can do away with subjective impressions.
An imperceptible inner transformation, the transfiguration of
your being, continues your whole life long. It makes each day
God's own today. It is, already on this earth, the beginning
of the resurrection, the dawning of a life that has no end.
Wonder of a love without beginning or end....

You will be surprised to find yourself saying: This Jesus,
the Risen Lord, was in me, and yet I didn't feel anything. So
often I looked for him elsewhere. As long as I kept fleeing

the living springs he had set in the hollow of my being, run as I might across the earth, far, very far, I was only going astray on paths that lead nowhere. A joy in God was impossible to find. But the time came when I discovered that Christ had never left me. I still did not dare to speak to him, yet he already had understood me, already he was speaking to me. Baptism had been the mark of an invisible presence. When the veil of worry lifted, the trusting of faith came and illuminated even my night.

— *Prayer: Seeking the Heart of God,* 43–45

Discover That Christ Is Present

Two of my brothers and I were in Ethiopia one day, during the Advent season. At Christmas, we visited a village of lepers. A woman named Adjebush told us her story. When she found out she had leprosy, her husband left her. Her four sons were fighting in the war; one had been killed, and she had no news of the others. Her little girl was sleeping beside her. Her deepest desire was that her daughter would understand the faith. With both legs amputated, Adjebush could not even go out to beg.

Then she spoke these unexpected words: "I weep inner tears and sometimes outer tears, but I know that Christ is here, standing beside me." And she began to praise God by lifting up her hands, according to the Coptic Orthodox tradition.

We asked ourselves: where does she get such trust? We realized that she drew it from the wellsprings of prayer. She had let a whole inner life develop within her; she had gone forward in a life of deep communion with God. Adjebush understood that suffering does not come from God.

She knew that God was not the author of her misfortunes and trials.

As she kept on praying, she began to comment on our visit to her, and her words turned into a kind of hymn on her lips. She said to God, "It's Christmas and they came to see me; it's Christmas and they did not stay home, they came here."

We were astonished to realize that often we perceive a unique, luminous Gospel insight in people who are totally destitute. All of us would like to be as close to God as that humble Ethiopian Orthodox woman. And all of us, like her, would like to discover in the simplicity of our hearts that Christ is present, close to us (see Mt 28:20b).

— *God Is Love Alone*, 44–45

Reading the Gospel

When we open the Gospel, each of us can say, "These words of Jesus are rather like a very ancient letter written in an unknown language. But since it is written to me by someone who loves me, I am going to try to understand its meaning, and to put into practice right away the little I have grasped.... "

No one is able to understand the entire Gospel in isolation from others. Each person has to say. "In this unique communion which is the Church, what I do not understand of the faith is understood by others who are living from it. I do not rely on my faith alone but on the faith of Christians of all times, those who have gone before us, from the time of Mary and the apostles to those of today. And day after day I prepare inwardly to put my trust in the mystery of faith."

— Introduction to *The New Testament: Selected Readings* (Fount, 1993), 8–9

From Doubt to Humble Trust

We are in a world where light and darkness coexist (see Jn 1:4–5 and 8:12).

As we aspire to the light, could a doubt take hold of us? A Russian believer, Dostoyevsky, far from worrying about this, wrote, "I am a child of doubt and unbelief. What terrible suffering it has cost me and still costs me, this longing to believe, which is so much the stronger in my soul as more arguments against it rise up within me.... My 'hosanna' has passed through the crucible of doubt."

And yet Dostoyevsky could continue, "There is nothing more beautiful, more profound, more perfect than Christ. Not only *is* there nothing, but there *can be* nothing."

When that man of God suggests that the nonbeliever coexists in him with the believer, his passionate love for Christ still remains undiminished.

Happy are those who walk from doubt toward the brightness of a humble trusting in Christ! Just like the sun dispelling the morning mist, light will shine in the nights of the soul. Not an illusory trust but a clear-headed one that impels us to act in the midst of real-life situations, to understand, to love.

Years ago, some of my brothers and I spent some time in Calcutta, in a district of great poverty. In the afternoons, Mother Teresa would sometimes ask me to go with her to the homes for the dying to visit lepers who were simply there waiting to die. And every morning, with one of my brothers who is a doctor, we went to take care of children who were seriously ill. It was a life-changing experience. Sometimes children even died in our arms.

From the very first day I took care of a little girl of four months; her mother had died shortly after she was born.

They told me it was likely that she would not live very long. Mother Teresa put her in my arms and entreated me to take her with me to Taizé so that she could receive proper care. And I said to myself: if that child were to sense the anxiety I feel for her life, what would become of her?

And I continued: let your anxiety be transformed into the trust of faith. As long as the child lives, entrust her to God. Resting on your heart, she will at least have experienced the happiness of trust in her short life.

When we arrived in Taizé, the brothers gathered in my room to see the child. I placed the little girl, named Marie, on my bed and, for the first time, she began to gurgle like a happy baby.

And in the end she lived. She grew up in my sister Genevieve's home. Today she is an adult. She is my god-daughter and I love her like a father.

—*God Is Love Alone*, 63–65

The Beauty of Common Prayer

A question has been preoccupying my brothers and myself for many years now: why do so many young people, in vast regions of the world, take part less and less in prayer in churches, or even not at all? Why do some say that they are bored when they attend a service of worship?

If Christ was not being deserted in this way in the communion of his Body, his Church, if there was not such an absence of young people in the churches, our community would not have been stimulated to welcome the young so that they could pray, share, and be listened to. And to welcome them not just in Taizé, but also during meetings in Europe or on different continents, including in places where some of our brothers share the life of the poor.

In Taizé or during these meetings, we have discovered that the beauty of a community prayer sung together can allow young people to let the desire for God well up in them, and also to enter into the depths of contemplative waiting.

Nothing is more conducive to a communion with the living God than a meditative common prayer with, as its high point, singing that never ends and that continues in the silence of one's heart when one is alone again. When the mystery of God becomes tangible through the simple beauty of symbols, when it is not smothered by too many words, then prayer with others, far from exuding monotony and boredom, awakens us to heaven's joy on earth.

— *God Is Love Alone,* 52–53

A Very Simple Prayer

Gospel realities can penetrate you through simple chants, sung over and over again: "Jesus, your light is shining within us; let my heart always welcome your love." When you work, when you rest, these realities keep echoing within you.

Sometimes prayer is an inner struggle, and sometimes it means surrendering one's whole being. At a given moment, it becomes simply resting in God in silence. That is perhaps one of the high points of prayer.

— *Prayer: Seeking the Heart of God,* 36

God Wants Us to Be Happy

For those who want to surrender themselves to Christ with steadfast hearts and give him their entire lives, there is a choice to be made, a decision to make. What decision? To let an unbounded gratefulness to God well up in us.

This gratefulness is a basic attitude. It is a peaceful joy always reawakened in us by the Holy Spirit (Lk 10:21). It is the spirit of praise. It attempts to view others and their aspirations with hopefulness.

God wants us to be happy. It is up to us to detect the Gospel realities that make life beautiful: trust, the spirit of praise, an overflowing heart, a joy renewed at every moment. . . .

In the New Testament, the apostle Peter assures us: "You love Christ although you have never seen him, and you believe in him though you still do not see him, so you are filled with a joy too deep for words that is already transfiguring you" (1 Pet 1:8).

And when fogs of hesitation arise, we are surprised to find ourselves saying, "We love you, Christ, perhaps not as we would like to, but we do love you. And what is most transparent in our lives is built up by a humble trusting in you."

— *Letter 1999–2001, 3–4*

The Holy Spirit, a Support and a Comfort

If Christ were not risen and if he had not sent his Holy Spirit, he would not be present with all people. He would simply be one more remarkable person in the history of humanity. But it would not be possible to converse with him. We would not dare to address him, "Christ Jesus, I rely on you at every moment. Even when I am unable to pray, you are my prayer."

Before leaving them, Christ assured his disciples that he would send them the Holy Spirit as a support and a comfort (see Jn 14:16–20). As a result we can make this discovery: just as Christ was present with his disciples on earth, so he continues through the Holy Spirit to be present for us today.

More easily grasped for some, more hidden for others, his mysterious presence is always there. It is as if we could hear him say, "Are you not aware that I am alongside you and, through the Holy Spirit, I live within you? I will never abandon you" (see Mt 28:20).

This mysterious presence is invisible to our eyes. For all of us, faith always remains a humble trust in Christ and the Holy Spirit. — *God Is Love Alone,* 17–18

Christ Is United to Every Human Being

A luminous Gospel insight reappeared during the Second Vatican Council. For a long time it had remained buried under the dust of the ages: "Christ is united to every human being without exception...." Later on, Pope John Paul II would add: "...even if they are not aware of it."

Every year, during a private audience, my desire is to gladden the heart of Pope John Paul II by sharing with him a hope that he caused us to discover. I have told him how much his striking intuition — Christ is united to every human being, even if they are not aware of it — could open onto an unclouded understanding of faith on earth.

Multitudes of human beings do not know that Christ is united to them and are unaware of the way he looks at every life with love. They know nothing about God, not even God's name. And yet God remains in communion with everyone. — *God Is Love Alone,* 16

Rejoice in Every Instant

One of the first brothers in our community has constantly said with simplicity, "I rejoice in every instant that I live." Like every human being, he has known trials. How can he rejoice in every instant? He knows what it means to remain faithful in a vocation as the years pass. He knows how to be attentive to what is essential and to return to it at every moment. That is what supports a joy. To go forward in a vocation, he also knows how important it is to have a short inner prayer that is often repeated. For many years he has been praying with these words: "Jesus, my joy, my hope, and my life." — *From Doubt to the Brightness of a Communion* (Letter, 1997), 15

A Love beyond All Comprehension

Do not be dismayed when the essential seems to remain hidden from your eyes. That only makes you more eager than ever to go on toward the One who is risen.

Day by day, you will sense more of the depth and the breadth of a love beyond all comprehension (Eph 3:18–19). From it, until life's end, you will draw wonder, and also the courage needed for new beginnings.

— *The Sources of Taizé*, 10

4

Love and Say It with Your Life

A Way of Reconciliation

One night, a man called Nicodemus came to visit Jesus. He learned from him that without "being born again" (Jn 3:1–8), no one can see the realities of God. Reconciliation and forgiveness are among those pure wellsprings that lead to a new birth.

Whoever seeks reconciliation with all their energy discovers that there is a "before" as well as an "after."

There is a "before" for those who, wounded by many humiliations, think: I will not manage to forgive and to be reconciled. But one day they start to consider: if I refuse forgiveness, what can I reflect of Christ?[1] As they come to have the desire for reconciliation, they are more concerned to understand others than to convince them by arguments.

And there is an "after" when, reconciled, they experience a new birth. And God comes to heal the secret wound of the soul.

---

1. When timidity keeps us from asking for forgiveness, why not dare to make a simple gesture that needs no words: extend your hand so that the other person can make in it the sign of forgiveness, the sign of the cross?

If we were to let ourselves be clothed in forgiveness as in a garment, we would glimpse a transfiguration of our being and the brightness of a communion.

If the love that forgives became a flame burning within us....

If compassionate hearts were at the beginning of everything....

...around us would shine, whether we knew it or not, a Gospel radiance....[2]

...and these words would be illuminated from within: "Love, and say it by your life!"[3]

> — From Doubt to the Brightness
> of a Communion (Letter, 1997), 3–4

Creators of Solidarity

Today more than ever before, a call is arising to open paths of trust even in humanity's darkest hours. Can we hear that call?

There are people who, by giving themselves, attest that human beings are not doomed to hopelessness. Are we among them?

More and more people throughout the world are becoming aware of how urgent it is to come to the aid of the victims of poverty, a poverty that is constantly on the rise. This is a basic necessity to make peace on earth possible.

---

2. Communicating Christ never means trying to impose oneself. The Gospel is not a vise that clamps down upon another person's conscience and entraps that person. A believer from Bangladesh, speaking about those around him who do not know Christ, said, "When you are near a fire, you are warmed. When the fire of God's love is in us, does it not shine on those who are close to us, even if we do not realize it?"

3. According to St. Augustine, fourth century.

The disparity between the accumulation of wealth by some and the poverty of countless others is one of the most serious questions of our time. Will we do all in our power for the world economy to provide solutions? Neither misfortunes nor the injustice of poverty come from God; all God can do is give his love. And so we are filled with astonishment when we discover that God looks at every human being with infinite tenderness and deep compassion.

When we realize that God loves us, that God loves even the most forsaken human being, then our hearts open to others. We are made more aware of the dignity of the human person and we ask ourselves: how can we prepare ways of trust on earth?

However powerless we may be, are we not called to communicate a mystery of hope to those around us by the lives we live?

— *Love and Say It with Your Life* (Letter, 2002), 1–2

Relieving the Suffering of the Littlest

In 1945, a young man from the region started an association to take care of children who had lost their families because of the war. He asked us to welcome a number of them in Taizé. A community of men could not take care of children. So I telephoned my sister Genevieve and asked her to come back for a time; the children needed a mother. An artist with all her being, she had undertaken advanced studies on the piano. She did not hesitate to answer yes, however. And gradually she realized that she could not leave those children, that she had to devote her life to them. At the beginning there were three of them; the months passed, and soon there were twenty or so. She set up home with them in an old house in the village.

Her whole life long, she lived in the same old house with other children as well, until they were grown up. They still come to stay with her today, bringing their own children and grandchildren. Later she welcomed Marie, the four-month-old baby that Mother Teresa entrusted to me in Calcutta to take care of, who grew up in her home.

Seeing the faithfulness of my sister Genevieve over the years, I have understood that it is above all kind-heartedness that has enabled her to weather so many events. Kind-heartedness is an invaluable stimulus to action.

— *God Is Love Alone*, 48–49

Love and Forgive

Prayer is a treasure of the Gospel. It opens a way forward which leads us to love and to forgive.

Forgiveness can change both our heart and our life: severity and harsh judgments recede and leave room in our hearts for goodness and kindness. And we become capable of seeking to understand rather than to be understood.

All who root their lives in forgiveness are able to pass through rock-hard situations like the water of a stream which, in early springtime, makes its way through the still-frozen ground.

However meager our resources, one of today's most urgent tasks is to bring about understanding where there are oppositions. Certain memories from the past are enough to keep individuals or nations apart.

Nothing is more tenacious than the memory of past wounds and humiliations. When we seek tirelessly to forgive and to be reconciled, a future opens up beyond all our expectations.

And what is true for each person is true as well in that mystery of communion which is the Body of Christ, his Church.   — *Astonished by Joy* (Letter, 2000), 2–3

A Man Named John

In the middle of the twentieth century there appeared a man named John, born in a humble peasant family in the north of Italy. When he announced the Second Vatican Council, that elderly man, John XXIII, pronounced words that are among the most crystal-clear imaginable: "We will not try to find out who was wrong, we will not try to find out who was right, we will only say: let us be reconciled!"

During the last meeting we had with him shortly before his death, three of us from our community were present. We understood how deeply John XXIII wished us to be at peace concerning the future of our vocation. Making circular gestures with his hands, he explained, "The Catholic Church is made up of ever larger concentric circles." Rather than giving in to worries, wasn't the essential already accomplished if we went forward in peace of heart?

                    — *Peace of Heart in All Things*, 56

The Eucharist, Source of Reconciliation

At the same period as Pope John XXIII, in Constantinople there was a man of the same prophetic vein, the Orthodox Patriarch Athenagoras. During a visit to him, what raised our hopes was the awareness that that eighty-six-year-old man — with so few means at his disposal and enmeshed in a complex political situation — could have an enormous impact both close at hand and far away. He had the greatness of the truly generous.

Until the day I die, I will see the patriarch as he was when we took our leave. Standing in the doorway, he lifted his hands as if he were offering the chalice at the Eucharist and repeated once again, "The cup and the breaking of the bread, there is no other way; remember.... "

— *Peace of Heart in All Things, 67*

Forgive and Then Forgive Again

You want to follow Christ, and not look back: are you going to make your way through life with a heart that is reconciled, even amid the most crippling tensions?

Suppose people distort your intentions. If you are judged wrongly (Mt 5:11–12) because of Christ, forgive. You will find that you are free, free beyond compare.

Forgive and then forgive again. That is the highest expression of loving (Mt 18:21–22). There you make yours the prayer of Jesus, "Forgive them, they do not know what they are doing" (Lk 23:34).

You forgive not in order to change the other person, but simply to follow Christ.

Consider your neighbors not just at one particular phase of their existence but through all the stages of their life.

Strive to be transparent. Have nothing to do with clever maneuvering. Never manipulate another's conscience, using their anxiety as a lever to force them into your way of thinking.

To be free of temptation, sing Christ's praises until you are joyful and serene.

His call is to joy, not to gloom.

At every age, forge ahead in faith. Even in days of grayness, his gift of cheerfulness, gaiety even. No lamenting, but

at every moment leave everything with him, even your body
worn out with fatigue. — *The Sources of Taizé,* 26

Simplicity Steeped in Clear-Sightedness

There is nothing naive about the spirit of childhood, about
simplicity according to the Gospel. They are inseparable
from discernment. They call for maturity. Far from being
simplistic, they are steeped in clear-sightedness.

— *Peace of Heart in All Things,* 15

Ways of Hope

I have been invited several times to Poland to take part in the
Silesian miners' pilgrimage at Piekary. Some of them go by
foot for four hours and then stand several hours more during
the prayer. The crowd is so enormous that you cannot take
it all in at one glance, even from the top of the hill. I have
been asked to talk to them about Mary:

"Not one of you Polish workers thinks you have an influence on the development of the human race. I want to tell
you that the contrary is true. It is not those who appear to
be in the front ranks who bring about changes in the world.

"Look at the Virgin Mary. Neither did she think that her
life was essential for the future of the human family. Like
the Mother of God, you are the humble people of this world
who are preparing the ways that lead to a future for every-
body. Your faithful waiting on God is carrying forward many
other people throughout the world."

— *His Love Is a Fire,* 103

Choose to Love

Like an almond tree that blossoms at the first hint of spring, a breath of trusting makes the deserts of the heart burst into flower again.

Borne forward by this breath, who would not wish to alleviate human suffering and trials? Even when our feet stumble along a stony path, who would not wish to put these Gospel words into practice in their life: "Whatever you do for the least, the most destitute, you are doing for me, Christ"? (Mt 25:40).

A century after Christ, a believer wrote, "Clothe yourself in cheerfulness. . . . Cleanse your heart of harmful sadness and you will live for God" (*The Shepherd of Hermas,* precept 42, 1 and 4).

Whoever lives for God chooses to love. Making such a choice one's own calls for unfailing vigilance.

A heart determined to love can radiate goodness without end. Its great concern is to relieve the torments of others nearby and far away.

All who live for God sense that their entire existence is staked on the trust they place in Christ and in the Holy Spirit.

If an inner fog were to make us drift away from the trusting of faith, Christ does not abandon us for all that. No one is excluded either from his love or from his forgiveness (see 1 Tim 2:4).

And if discouragement and even doubts arise within us, Christ does not love us any the less. He is there, shedding light on our path. And his call rings out: "Come, follow me!" (Mk 10:21).

How often, during a private conversation with a young person, do I hear this question: How can I be myself? How can I fulfil myself? Some people are preoccupied by this to the point of anguish. Then I think of what one of my brothers once said: Christ does not say to me, "Be yourself." He says, "Be with me." Christ does not tell us, "Find yourself." He says, "You, follow me!"   — *God Is Love Alone, 29–30*

One and the Same Source

The more you draw creative energies from prayer, the more you will discover a capacity to build together with others. Can you sense that struggle and contemplation have one and the same source? If you pray, it is out of love. If you struggle, taking on responsibilities to make the world more fit to live in, that too is for love.   — *Taizé: Trust on Earth*, 20

Reconciliation without Delay

My mother's mother was a woman of courage. During the First World War her three sons were fighting at the front. She was a widow and she lived in the north of France, where they were under shell-fire. But she insisted on staying, so that she could open her home to refugees — old people, children, pregnant women. She did not leave till the last minute when everyone had to flee. Then she went to the Dordogne.

She was penetrated by the deep desire that never again would anyone have to go through what she had experienced. In Europe, divided Christians were killing one another; let them at least be reconciled, to prevent another war.

She came from old Protestant stock: in the house where my mother was born, guests were still shown the secret chamber where in times past the pastor was hidden during periods of persecution. To bring about an immediate reconciliation within herself, she used to go to a Catholic church.

It was as if she had known intuitively that, in the Catholic Church, the Eucharist was a source of unanimity of the faith.

The miracle of her life was that in reconciling within herself the stream of her original faith with the Catholic faith, she did not become a symbol of repudiation for her family.

She arrived at my parents' a year or so later. Worn out with fatigue, she fainted as she entered our house. They carried her away in a red blanket. I can see the scene as if it had just taken place.

This made a great impact on me and something irreversible took place. Those two gestures of hers — taking in the most distressed and achieving reconciliation within oneself — had a lifelong effect upon me. . . .

Mothers or grandmothers can rejoice. Their acts of faithfulness sometimes leave traces whose total results will never be seen in their lifetimes.

— *And Your Deserts Shall Flower,* 52–53

Living in Communion

For two thousand years Christ has been present through the Holy Spirit, and his mysterious presence is made tangible in a visible communion[4] that brings together women, men, and young people who are called to go forward together, without separating from one another.[5]

And yet throughout their history Christians have experienced many upheavals: separations have arisen between those who nonetheless professed faith in the same God of love.

---

4. That communion is called the Church. In the heart of God, the Church is one; it cannot be divided.

5. The closer we come to the Gospel, the closer we come to one another. And the separations that tear us apart draw to an end.

Reestablishing communion is urgent today; it cannot continually be put off until later, until the end of time.[6] Will we do all we can for Christians to wake up to the spirit of communion?[7]

There are Christians who, without waiting, are already in communion with one another in the places where they live, quite humbly, quite simply.

Through their own life, they would like to make Christ present for many others. They know that the Church does not exist for itself but for the world, to place within it a ferment of peace.

"Communion" is one of the most beautiful names of the Church. In it, there can be no harsh words exchanged but only transparency, heartfelt kindness, compassion . . . and the gates of holiness swing open.

— *A Future of Peace* (Letter, 2005), 3–4

Sing to Christ until We Are Joyful and Serene

Following Christ with a steadfast heart does not mean lighting fireworks that flare up brightly and then go out. It means setting out, and then remaining, on a road of trust that can last our whole life long.

---

6. Christ calls us to be reconciled without delay. We cannot forget his words in the Gospel according to St. Matthew: "When you are offering your gift at the altar, if you remember that your brother or sister has something against you, first go and be reconciled" (5:23). "First go" not "Put it off till later."

7. In Damascus, in the Middle East beset by trials, there lives the Greek Orthodox patriarch of Antioch, Ignatius IV. He has written these striking words: "The ecumenical movement is going backward. What remains of the prophetic event of the early days incarnated in figures like Pope John XXIII and Patriarch Athenagoras? Our divisions make Christ unrecognizable; they are contrary to his will to see us be one 'so that the world may believe.' We have an urgent need for prophetic initiatives in order to bring ecumenism out of the twists and turns in which I fear it is getting stuck. We have an urgent need for prophets and saints to help our churches to be converted by mutual forgiveness."

This trust always remains humble. If faith became a spiritual pretension it would lead nowhere.

A breath of trusting can be held back by tormenting memories of a recent or distant past. The Gospel encourages us not to look back (Lk 9:62), not to linger over our failures.

Endless discussions with ourselves can clutter our being and keep peace of heart far away. At such times it takes courage to say to Christ, "Inner Light, do not let my darkness speak to me!"[8]

Gospel joy, the spirit of praise, will always involve an inner decision.

Daring to sing to Christ until we are joyful and serene... (see Phil 4:6–7; Eph 5:19). Not with just any kind of joy, but with that joy that comes straight from the wellsprings of the Gospel.   — *God Is Love Alone*, 31

A Future of Peace

"God has plans for a future of peace for you, not of misfortune; God wants to give you a future and a hope" (see Jer 29:11 and 39:17).

Today, a great many people are longing for a future of peace, for humanity to be freed from threats of violence.

If some are gripped by worry about the future and find themselves at a standstill, there are also young people all over the world who are inventive and creative.

These young people do not let themselves be caught up in a spiral of gloom. They know that God did not create us to be passive. For them, life is not subject to a blind destiny. They are aware that skepticism and discouragement have the power to paralyze human beings.

---

8. St. Augustine, *Confessions*, XII, 10.

And so they are searching, with their whole soul, to prepare a future of peace and not of misfortune. More than they realize, they are already making of their lives a light that shines around them.

Some are bearers of peace and trust in situations of crisis and conflict. They keep going even when trials or failures weigh heavily on their shoulders.

On some summer evenings in Taizé, under a sky laden with stars, we can hear the young people through our open windows. We are constantly astonished that there are so many of them. They search; they pray. And we say to ourselves: their aspirations to peace and trust are like these stars, points of lights that shine in the night.

— *A Future of Peace* (Letter, 2005), 1–2

Let Your Soul Live!

In simple prayer, many people understand one day that God is calling them. What is God's call?

God wants us to prepare ourselves to be bearers of joy and peace.

Will we listen to God when his words ring out in us: "Don't stop; keep going forward; let your soul live!"

Then we may realize that we have been created to head toward something infinite, something absolute. And we can make this discovery: it is sometimes in demanding situations that human beings become most fully themselves.

When we are supported by one another[9] and do not let ourselves be brought to a halt by obstacles, when we know

---

9. Isolation leads to discouragement and does not allow the gifts of each person to blossom. For years now, we have been inviting the young to take part in a "pilgrimage of trust on earth" as a way of helping them to be supported by one another. It enables them to realize that they are linked to many other young people

where to find the courage to keep going forward, then we realize that there is heartfelt joy, and even sheer happiness, in responding to God's call. Yes, God wants happiness for us!

And then something we never dared hope for appears. We leave behind us the long nights with hardly a glimmer of light. Walking at times along ways of darkness, instead of weakening us, can even build us up within.

What means most to us is going from one discovery to another. Welcoming the coming day as God's today. Searching for peace of heart in all things. And life becomes beautiful ... yes, life will be beautiful.

—*A God Who Simply Loves* (Letter, 2003), 4

---

by a common search for God, by a common hope, and by complementary commitments. We have done this, moreover, without creating an organized movement around our community of Taizé.

5

Christ Comes to Light Up
Our Nights

Do You Recognize the Way of Hope?

Are there realities in the Gospel that make life beautiful?
Yes, there are. And one of these is hope. It enables us to
go beyond discouragements and even to rediscover a zest
for life.

And where is its source? It lies in the audacity of a life of
communion in God. But how is this communion possible?
God loved us first (see 1 Jn 4:10, 19). God seeks us tirelessly,
even if we are unaware of it (see Lk 15:4–10).

Trust, hope, and peace of heart are rooted in a mysterious presence, the presence of Christ. By the Holy Spirit he is
there in each person, like someone who is humble of heart.
And his voice says softly, "Do you recognize the way of hope
that is open for you?"

Then how can we keep from saying to Christ, "I would
like to follow you for my entire lifetime, but do you know
how weak I am?" Through the Gospel he replies, "I am familiar with your trials and your poverty. To remain faithful
your whole life long, you think you have nothing, or almost

nothing. But you are filled. Filled by what? By the presence of the Holy Spirit. His compassion illuminates even the shadows of your soul" (see Rev 2:9).

— *God Is Love Alone,* 12–13

A Prospect of Happiness?

If we could realize that a life of happiness is possible, even in hours of darkness.... [1]

What makes life happy is to head toward simplicity: simplicity of our heart, and of our life.

For a life to be beautiful, extraordinary abilities or great expertise are not required. There is happiness in the humble giving of oneself.

When simplicity is closely linked to kind-heartedness,[2] then even people without resources can create a space of hope around themselves.

Yes, God wants happiness for us![3] But he never invites us to remain passive, or indifferent to the suffering of others.[4]

---

1. Among the first words of Christ on earth we find these: "Happy the simple in heart... happy those who weep, they will be comforted... happy the merciful, mercy will be shown to them..." (see Mt 5:1–12). See also Dt 4:40.

2. Simplifying never means choosing a harsh, judgmental attitude devoid of generosity. The spirit of simplicity shines out in kind-heartedness. Our brothers in Taizé, as well as those who live on other continents among the very poor, are aware that we are called to a great simplicity of life. We have discovered that, sometimes with very limited means, we can be enabled to offer a hospitality we did not believe ourselves capable of.

3. The writer Dostoyevsky, an Orthodox Christian, wrote, "I know that men can be happy without losing the ability to live on earth. I do not want to believe, and I cannot believe, that evil is the normal condition of men" (from *A Writer's Journal*).

4. The philosopher Paul Ricoeur, a Protestant Christian, writes, "I have nothing to reply to those who say, 'There is too much evil in the world for me to believe in God.' God does not want us to suffer. From being all-powerful, God becomes 'all-loving.' God's only power is unarmed love. God has no other power than to love and, when we are suffering, to address a word of assistance to us. Our difficulty is to be able to hear it."

On the contrary, God encourages us to be creators, and to manage to create even in times of trial.

Our life is not subject to the whims of fate or to a blind destiny. Far from it! Our life finds meaning when it is above all the living response to a call from God.

— A Prospect of Happiness? (Letter, 2001), 1

God's Call

How can we recognize such a call and discover what God wants from us?

God wants us to be a reflection of his presence, bearers of a Gospel hope.[5]

There are people who perceive, however faintly at first, that God's call for them is a vocation for their entire lifetime.

The Holy Spirit has the strength to sustain a yes for our whole life. Has he not placed in us a desire for eternity and the infinite?

In the Spirit, at every age, it is possible to find new vitality and to say to ourselves, "Be steadfast of heart, and keep going forward!" (Sir 2:2).

And then, by his mysterious presence, the Holy Spirit brings about a change in our hearts, rapidly for some, imperceptibly for others. What had been obscure or even disturbing starts to become clear. Until the end of our days, a yes spoken in trust can bring so much clarity.

Although we are called to make the gift of ourselves, we are not really built for such a gift. Christ understands our inner resistances. By overcoming them, we demonstrate our love to him.   *— A Prospect of Happiness?* (Letter, 2001), 2

---

5. It is possible to discover God in particular through the lives of those who, often without realizing it, are a reflection of God among human beings.

A Few Simple Truths

People who strive to surrender themselves to God body and soul let themselves be built up from within on the basis of a few simple truths from the Gospel. Truths which at one time or another have touched them to the core. Why not summarize them briefly so that they can be called to mind at any moment?

The fruit of much thought, matured slowly and worked out over a long period of time, this summary most often takes shape in the midst of life's struggles. Once we have found it, it can carry us forward our whole life long.

This does not mean a great many words, but a few essential Gospel values that are concise and clear enough for us to return to them again and again. If we forget them for a time, we can return to them again the very moment that they come to mind.   — *His Love Is a Fire,* 21

God Cannot but Give His Love

Christ Jesus did not come to earth to judge the world, but so that through him every human creature might be saved, reconciled. Six centuries after Christ, a Christian thinker, St. Isaac of Nineveh, wrote these words: "God cannot but give his love."

Never, never indeed, is God a tormentor of the human conscience. He buries our past in the heart of Christ. God comes to weave our life like a beautiful garment, with the warm threads of his compassion.

And communion with him commits us in his name to lighten the distress of the innocent and to undertake responsibilities to reduce the suffering on earth.

And when we lighten the trials of others, it is Christ, the Risen One, whom we meet. He says of himself: "Whatever you do to the least of my brothers or sisters, you are doing it to me" (Mt 25:40).   — *Taizé: Trust on Earth,* 10

Letting Yourself Be Loved by God

For many years now, some of my brothers have been living in Bangladesh, sharing the life of the most destitute. One of them wrote me: "Our life has been deeply affected by the cyclone and the floods. Some of our neighbors ask us: Why all these misfortunes? Have we sinned so much?"

Often in the human heart there dwells a secret fear: God is going to punish me. When she was five years old, my little goddaughter Marie-Sonaly came to me one day in tears. Her adopted mother was in the hospital and the little girl said to me, "My mummy is sick; it's my fault. I hugged her too hard." Where do these guilt feelings come from, already so early in life?

To think that God punishes human beings is one of the greatest obstacles to faith. When God is seen as a tyrannical judge, St. John reminds us in letters of fire: "God is love. We are not the ones who loved God; God loved us. Let us love, because God loved us first." That is where everything begins: letting yourself be loved by God. But it's not so simple.... Why is it that some Christians find it so hard to believe that they are loved? They say to themselves: God loves others, but not me.

Human beings are sometimes severe. God, for his part, comes to clothe us in compassion. He weaves our life, like a beautiful garment, with the threads of his forgiveness. He buries our past in the heart of Christ and he has already taken care of our future.

God loves you before you love him. You think you are not waiting for him, and he is waiting for you. You say "I am not worthy," and he places on your finger the ring of the prodigal son. That is how the Gospel turns things upside down.

We are all prodigals! In the depths of your captivity, you turn toward God, and bitterness disappears from your face. God's forgiveness inspires your own singing. And the contemplation of God's forgiveness becomes a radiant kindness in the simple hearts that let themselves be led by the Spirit.

— *Prayer: Seeking the Heart of God*, 28–29

There Is No Violence in God

In the presence of physical violence or moral torture a question plagues us: If God is love, where does evil come from?

No one can explain the why of evil. In the Gospel, Christ enters into solidarity with the incomprehensible suffering of the innocent; he weeps at the death of someone he loves (Jn 11:35–36).

Did not Christ come to earth so that every human being might know that he or she is loved?[6] When we can sense hardly anything of God's presence, what good is agonizing over it?

It is enough to have the desire to welcome God's love for a flame to be kindled, little by little, in the secret recesses of our being.   — *The Wonder of a Love* (Letter, 1995), 1

---

6. "There is no violence in God. God sent Christ not to accuse us, but to call us to himself, not to judge us, because he loves us" (Letter to Diognetus, second century AD).

Let the Simple Heart Rejoice!

Three thousand years ago, Elijah, the believer, set out in search of a place where he could listen to God. He climbed a mountain in the wilderness. A hurricane arose, the earth began to shake, a conflagration broke out. Elijah knew that God was not in these outbursts of nature. God is never the author of earthquakes or natural disasters. Then everything became quiet and there was the murmur of a gentle breeze. Elijah covered his face. He had come to the realization that God's voice also made itself understood in a breath of silence.

One day we visited the leper hospital with Mother Teresa. I saw a leper raise his emaciated arms and begin to sing these words: "God has not inflicted a punishment on me; I praise him because my illness has turned into a visit from God." In his affliction, that man also had the intuition that suffering does not come from God.

God is not the author of evil. But he has accepted a huge risk. He wanted us to be creators with him. He wanted human beings not to be like passive robots, but free to decide personally on the direction their lives will take, free to love or not to love.

And Christ never stands by passively while someone suffers. Risen from the dead, he accompanies each of us in our suffering to such an extent that there is a pain God suffers, a pain Christ suffers. And, in his name, he enables us to share the distress of those who are undergoing incomprehensible trials; he leads us to alleviate the misery of the innocent.

Although human distress does not come from God, afterward some people discover that they have been purified by their trials. To understand this, it is necessary to have gained maturity and also to have crossed inner deserts. I would like to give an example. In February 1991 I was in the Philippines for a gathering of young people that my brothers had been preparing for several months. I paid a visit to an elderly woman, Aurora Aquino. Many years before, her son Benigno had spent seven years in prison; then he was exiled. When he was able to return to his country, he was assassinated just as he was getting off the plane. At the time, I had noticed a photograph of Aurora Aquino in a newspaper. Her face was that of a mother filled with compassion.

Conversing with Aurora Aquino, I discovered that, at the age of eighty-one, she had no bitterness in her heart. She even spoke these surprising words: trials purify us. I was not astonished to find in her such great selflessness. She is one of those elderly persons of whom we can say: for whoever knows how to love, for whoever knows how to suffer, life is filled with serene beauty.

Affected by the shock of some event, might you be undergoing the great trial, that of a broken relationship? Or again, despised and humiliated, have your purest intentions been distorted?

Humble prayer comes to heal the secret wound of the soul. And the mystery of human suffering is transfigured. The Spirit of the living God breathes upon what is destitute and fragile. In our wounds he causes living water to spring up. Through him the valley of tears becomes a place of living springs.

Let the simple heart rejoice! From peace of heart a Gospel joy can spring up, spontaneously.

— Prayer: Seeking the Heart of God, 29–31

The Transfiguration of Our Being Goes Forward Step by Step

Even if at times we seem to be in the night, a light is shining in the midst of the darkness. The apostle Peter invites us to focus our eyes on that light "until day begins to dawn and the sun rises in our hearts" (2 Pet 1:19).

A plant not turned toward the light withers away. If believers were to linger in the shadows, could trust grow within their hearts?

The Gospel comes to turn our lives upside down: by the Holy Spirit, Christ penetrates what worries us about ourselves. He reaches what seemed to be out of reach, so that even the darkest places can be illuminated by his presence.

When the night becomes dark, his love is a fire (see Ex 13:21–22). It causes what had been smoldering under the ashes to burst into flame. Christians like St. John of the Cross and St. Teresa of Avila began a new life of faith fairly late in life. They spoke of the fire that was often kindled with all the thorns of their past.

Marie Noël, a twentieth-century French poet of profound faith, wrote along the same lines: "The best and most nourishing souls are made of a few great and radiant acts of goodness and a thousand tiny obscure miseries which feed their goodness, like the wheat that lives from the decomposition of the soil."

One evening, during a prayer in a cathedral in Belgium full of young people, one of them asked me this question, "Brother Roger, show us the way to God!"

I replied: I don't know if I can show the way to God. But, in my old age, I can share a personal experience that has marked my entire life.

When I was young I was an invalid for many years, the result of tuberculosis followed by a serious relapse. I had time to read, to meditate, and to discover God's call: a vocation that could last for a lifetime.

When death seemed close, I sensed that, even more than the body, it is the depths of the self that are in need of healing. And our hearts are healed above all by a humble trust in God.

Those years of illness allowed me to realize that the source of happiness is not in prestigious talents or great expertise, but in the humble giving of oneself, yes the quite humble giving of oneself, in order to understand others with kind-heartedness.

Little by little, I realized that creative energies could arise even from a childhood or an adolescence that had been humiliated. The apostle Paul expresses this Gospel reality with great intuition when he writes, "It is when I am weak that I am made strong in God" (2 Cor 12:10).

And Christ can bring out of these trials a great boldness to create in God, to run the risks of faith. He passes through our limits, failures, and inner nights. He transforms them, he transfigures them throughout our lifetime.

An imperceptible inner change, the transfiguration of our being goes forward step by step. It is the beginning of a life that will know no end, already here on this earth.

When we are racked by the awareness of our limits or feelings of inferiority, we are surprised to find that Christ enables us to set out again with new energy.

The elderly Pope John XXIII passed through times of trial and used to say, "I am like a bird singing in a thorn bush." We too would like to communicate joy despite the thorns that prick us. Not just any kind of joy, but the joy that consists in knowing that Christ loves every human being as if that person were the only one (see Gal 2:20b).

God enables us to be born and reborn in him when we welcome his trust and his forgiveness into our lives. If we let ourselves be clothed in forgiveness as in a garment, we will glimpse a light shining in our night.

— *God Is Love Alone*, 38–41

By What Sign Can You Recognize That You Have Encountered Him?

Your aspiration is to follow Christ. By what sign can you recognize that you have encountered him? When, as you search for him in prayer, your inner struggles do not harden you but lead you to the very wellsprings of his love. And a way forward takes shape: it always leads from worries toward trusting in God.   — *Peace of Heart in All Things*, 81

"Seek and You Will Find"

It can happen that God seems to become distant. Some people are disconcerted by the impression that God is silent. Could the trusting of faith consist in saying "yes" to God's love even if there is this deep silence within us? (see Ps 42:3 and 5). Faith is like a surge of trusting repeated a thousand times over in the course of our life.

We need to remember that it is not our faith that creates God, and it is not our doubts that can cast him into nothingness. Even were we to feel no apparent resonance, the mysterious presence of Christ never disappears (see Mt 28:20). Although we may have the impression of an absence, there is above all the wonder of his continual presence.

When worries succeed in distancing us from the trusting of faith, some people ask themselves: have I become a nonbeliever? No, they are gaps of unbelief, nothing more.

The Gospel invites us to place our trust in Christ again and yet again, and to find in him a life of contemplation (see Mt 28:20). And Christ speaks these Gospel words to each of us: "Seek, seek and you will find" (Mt 7:7).

Happy those who walk from doubt toward humble trusting! When my mother was already very elderly, one day she spoke to me about her own mother and said, "You may not know that your grandmother, whom we loved and admired so much, did not find it easy to believe." "I did know it," I replied, "and I love her all the more for it."

My grandmother went through great trials. Her three brothers died of tuberculosis, and her father too. Then later on, one of her sons died. She used to write notes in her Bible. I found there this prayer to God: "I am not made for struggles.... I have doubts.... Help me!" And then these words: "Lord, we are unable to wage this struggle, but that is a reason for not leaving you, for remaining close to you."

For my part, I can say that when I was young, at a certain moment my faith seemed to be shaken. I did not really call into question the existence of God. What I doubted was the possibility of living in communion with him. I wanted to be so honest that there were times when I no longer dared to pray. I thought that I needed to know God in order to pray.

One fine day, when I was still young, I opened an old book and my eyes fell on some lines written in archaic French. The author wrote that although God was not communicable, Christ made him known: "Christ is the resplendence of God." I never forgot that. It is Christ who enables us to understand that God loves us (Jn 17:26).

In the summer of 1937 Lily, one of my seven sisters, the one to whom I had dictated my childhood poems and to whom I was very attached, fell seriously ill. She was the mother of five children. I realized that she was expected to die. Then I was able to say a prayer, these words of a psalm: "My heart says of you: seek his face. I am seeking your face, O God" (Ps 27:8). Those words seemed honest to me. I was able to kneel down and say that prayer. I realized that faith was in me and that it could be nothing other than a quite humble trust in God.   — *God Is Love Alone*, 65–67

Light in Our Nights

Sometimes I wonder why this trust in Christ who comes to illuminate our night is so essential for me. And I realize that this comes from a childhood experience.

During the weeks before Christmas, I used to spend lots of time in front of a manger scene looking at the Virgin Mary and the newborn infant at her feet. Such a simple image marks one for life. It enables us to realize one day that, through Christ, God himself came to be with us.

On Christmas Eve, we would go to church. When I was five or six years old, we lived in a mountain village, and the ground was covered with snow. Since I was the youngest, my father took me by the hand. My mother, my elder brother, and my seven sisters followed behind. My father showed me, in the clear sky, the shepherds' star that the wise men had seen.

Those moments come to my mind when I hear the reading from the apostle Peter: "Fix your eyes on Christ as on a star shining in the night, until the day dawns and the morning rises in your hearts" (2 Pet 1:19).

— *God Is Love Alone*, 19–20

6

Pages from the Journal

A priest whom I have never met wrote me a letter, which I pinned up on the wall of my room. It has been there for many years now; every now and again I stop to read it: "Today I celebrate the tenth anniversary of my ordination. I could not help thinking of you and your community. Together, we are all trying to scale the same mountain, though by different paths, toward Christ.

"I remembered a little short-cut which perhaps will help us to be together a little sooner. This short-cut is for us to be children in spirit.

"I firmly believe that this is the way we shall achieve unity. The final union will take place in an atmosphere of childhood, with humility, simplicity, confidence, and complete trust.

"This path, this way, I would like humbly and simply to bring to your notice, today." — *Violent for Peace*, 101

April 13, 1969

Once again, a youth asks what prayer can be for him. To begin with, I tell him, "Do not look for a solution that fails to take your humanity into account. Personally, without my body I should have no idea of how to pray. I am no angel, and I have no complaint about that. At certain periods I sense that I pray more with my body than with my understanding. Such prayer is at ground level — on one's knees, or bowing low, looking at the place where the Eucharist is celebrated, taking advantage of the peaceful silence and even of the sounds coming up from the village. The body is well and truly present to listen, grasp, love. It would be sheer folly to want to leave it out of account!" — *Festival* *

May 10, 1969

It is good to write each day and if necessary to oblige myself to do so. It is my handwork, as someone else pounds dough and makes bread. It is the means of a fundamental independence.

May 15, 1969

The fascination of the sky, gray or dazzling, is with me as soon as I wake. It is something that is a dominant characteristic of many people who were born in the country. Rapidly rise to see what the weather is like. Light rain has dampened the ground. The trees on the terrace are gleaming under the cool rain. The lemon-balm is in bud, about to burst open. The sky is low but the earth sings.

August 5, 1969

Night of the Transfiguration — festival of the present age. Our century has uncovered depths in humankind so vast that

---

*Journal entries from April 1969 through February 1970 are taken from *Festival*.

they sum up the whole of humanity, from its origins until now. But to these vast spaces underlying the human person is offered a transfiguration.

January 10, 1970

The race to succeed, to get ahead at all costs: what devastation this is for Christians! When people have no other means of regaining confidence in themselves, they are doomed to dislocation and empty away the best of themselves.

February 1, 1970

All through the day, wherever I am and whoever I may be talking to, I find ways of watching what is happening in the sky. The sight of creativity constantly in action, so many shades of gold set off by brilliant grays — joyfulness wells up inside me; it is not so hard to bear the burden of contradictions.

February 9, 1970

During a conversation in the church, a young man, sitting fairly far back, asked me timidly: "Brother, who, for you, is Christ?" I have never been asked that in public before. I ask him his name. He is called Alain, and comes from the local mining region. I suggest that he repeat the question in the microphone. He expresses himself anew, in a strong local accent.

For me, Christ is he by whom I live, but also the one for whom I, with you, am searching.

June 26, 1970

This afternoon Bernard, a young man from a nearby village, was ordained priest in the church at St. Gengoux. Since time immemorial no one has been ordained in these parts. I recall the welcome I received from the priest of this same village thirty years ago, how from the first moment he gave me his trust. At that time his church was always practically empty — it seemed as though everything had been extinguished forever. He too was giving help to political refugees. I live anew one of our first encounters: Emmanuel Mounier happened to be passing through Taizé and the two of us cycled over to see him. We were both enthralled: lost in this isolated corner, he was full of attention for all that was happening. — *Struggle and Contemplation**

July 3, 1970

Engineers taking a refresher course in information processing share our supper. An atheist among them vigorously contests all that Christians believe. His scientific mind gauges everything by what he can know. At the end of the evening I tell him: "The questions you have been asking are questions that a man living by the certainty of God also dares to keep asking himself during his life. This kind of questioning, part of our basic doubt, does not prevent us from constantly setting out from doubt toward belief."

---

*Journal entries from June 1970 through March 1972 are taken from *Struggle and Contemplation*.

July 26, 1970

In the mail comes a postcard of the front of a church illuminated in the night. On the back a message, "Thank you for the night-light." The child who wrote it was beside me with the other children for several days. Puzzling and uncommunicative. No response until one day, questioning him, I discovered that he was afraid of the dark. At the next service I gave him a night-light for his bedroom. All the children close to me each day! If they only knew how much their waiting for Christ supports our own!

August 10, 1970

I was brought up in the old traditions, but listening to younger people and sharing in their private struggles rids me of certain reflexes of fear. Without these thousands of young people here on the hill, where would I be now, in spite of my desire to be open?

August 20, 1970

Human beings only create by drawing on their poverty. I am well placed to assert that today: it is exactly thirty years ago that I discovered Taizé.

November 1, 1970

I love my room, with its orange walls, the floor of wide pine planks and the ceiling of painted beams. Some of us have a larger room, others a smaller. Some sleep on a mattress laid on the floor and have nothing but a table and a cupboard; others prefer to have more color around them. For each of us, once the door is shut, there awaits the same solitude. Of course, there is the kitchen where we find others around eleven in the evening, to talk and hear what is happening. Then each returns to his room and closes the door. Our yes to Christ for life means making this gesture every evening. Sometimes it costs. But this solitude is not to seek one's own self. . . . As the years pass, it opens us to the unique reality, Christ our first love.

November 21, 1970

Words of a little girl who lost her mother a few years ago: "When you own a lot of things, you are rich, but when you do not have all that, perhaps you are rich in love."

June 4, 1971

Splendor of my room in the early working hours. A warm light, objects clearly defined, the coolness of the air scarcely warmed since the night. People go to the far ends of the earth in search of what is offered very close at hand.

March 18, 1972

One of my brothers was speaking of that voice that doubts and mutters within us, "O yes, God chooses so-and-so, but I have nothing to make him consider me, my prayer is never more than a projection of myself." He remarked: is that really humility? It is almost, and yet it is just the opposite. It is simply a form of exaggerated love of self, a love turned into hatred. Now self-hate is closer to pride than to humility. If we refuse to believe, even just a little, in our love for God, we shall be unable to believe in his love for us.

April 5, 1972

I would go to the ends of the earth if necessary, to the farthest reaches of the globe, to speak over and over again of my confidence in the new generations, my confidence in the young.

We who are older have to listen, and not condemn. Listen, to grasp the creative intuitions alive within them. They are blazing trails, they are overturning barriers, they will take the whole People of God along with them. The young will find a way beyond the demarcation lines that now divide believers from believers, they will invent means of communion uniting believers with nonbelievers.

As for the old, I am convinced that without them the world would not be worth living in. Those societies, families, or churches that exclude them do not know what they are doing. Old people who accept their approaching death acquire irreplaceable powers of intuition. They understand with the understanding of the heart. By their loving trust they make it possible for the young, and the not-so-young, to become truly themselves; with their ability to discern the best in others, they release unsuspected sources of life in them.

Every rift between generations works against the sense of the universal.   — A Life We Never Dared Hope For*

April 8, 1972

With one of my brothers, I called on Father Buisson. His face shines with peace and mercy; he is gazing at the invisible already.

---

*Journal entries from April 1972 through December 1973 are taken from A Life We Never Dared Hope For.

Whoever would have thought it? He is eighty-six, and in a way he has replaced John XXIII in my life. At the age of forty, he still could not make up his mind to be ordained, so strong were his scruples, his feelings of guilt and inferiority. "That taught me to understand the people who come to unburden their souls to me."

Still listening, I rise to do what he can no longer do himself: taking three glasses from the cupboard, I pour out the sweet wine and pass round the few biscuits he buys for us when we come.

He asserts that, as far as he can see, his ministry has borne no fruit. When God takes him back to himself, he will know all that his priesthood has achieved.

May 23, 1972

Tuesday after Pentecost. A highway accident a few kilometers away has cost a boy his life.

After the midday prayer, I went to see the driver of the minibus; he was sitting in a corner of the church on a low stool. His eyes were bright, clear as deep waters before a storm. Neither of us spoke. I stood there with one hand resting on his bowed head. The other people who had been in the bus when the accident happened gradually gathered round; they had not been told that Hans-Peter had died on the way to the hospital. But as they came up, our silence made them realize. I began to pray, with others following in a long, restrained litany.

Later they explained that Hans-Peter, a seventeen-year-old electrical engineer, had only very recently found his way to the faith. The boy who had been driving the bus was the one who had been closest to him during that time.

June 4, 1972

After today's showers the air is cool, refreshing the very soul. Over on the hills toward Tournus, the gentle evening light changes from moment to moment. Down in the valley, cars speeding along: all homeward bound.

July 7, 1972

This day, Patriarch Athenagoras enters the life of eternity. With him we lose a man of the same prophetic vein as John XXIII. He had no lack of trials in his final years. He had realized what changes were necessary in the People of God, but with the situation as it was, he was obliged to suppress the best of his intuitions.

Nevertheless, he was always optimistic. "In the evening, when I retire to my room," he told me once, "I close the door on all my cares, and I say: Tomorrow!"

I cannot forget our last visit to him in Constantinople, two years ago. As we took our leave, standing in the doorway and making with his hands the gesture of raising the chalice, he said: "The cup and the breaking of bread. There is no other solution; remember."

Engraved on my memory, too, is a pilgrimage Max and I made with him around Constantinople during an earlier visit. Every time our car passed a spot where a Christian had died for Christ, he asked the driver to slow down or stop. We made the sign of the cross, then drove on.

July 15, 1972

The essential is always hidden from our eyes...and that lends still more ardor to the quest and sustains our advance toward the only reality.

This thought, much in my mind these past few days, might make a good heading for my next book....

March 4, 1973

In church this morning, after I had talked with a number of people, a little girl came up and asked, "Could you teach me how to confess?" There was a burden weighing on her frail shoulders. How can an eight-year-old child be so imprisoned in guilt? "Who can condemn us, since Jesus is praying for us?" I intend to make my Easter morning sermon a meditation on those words.

March 7, 1973

Discussed the meaning of Lent with a young pastor, who is spending a few days in retreat here. Lent: forty days granted us in which to marvel at a love too great for words.

July 10, 1973

Once again, during a private conversation, I hear a familiar question: How can I be myself? How can I fulfil myself? Those questions preoccupy some people to the point of anguish.

I remember what one of my brothers once said, talking of his encounter with Jesus: "He does not say, 'Be yourself.' He says, 'Be with me.'" How right he is! Christ does not tell us, "Find yourself" or "Run after yourself." He says, "You, follow me."

If "being oneself" means dropping our masks, giving up conformist attitudes and conventions, who would disagree? That is not just good, it is vital.

On the other hand, a person is chasing illusions if, in the quest to be himself, his ego asserts itself at the expense of others.

When the Gospel asks people to be themselves and develop their gifts and talents a hundredfold, it is not in order to serve their own ends, it is to serve others. In the Gospel, to be oneself means searching deeply until the irreplaceable gift given to each one of us is revealed. Through that special gift, unlike anyone else's, each person is brought to fulfillment in God.

July 16, 1973

Yesterday evening, I paused for a long time beside the oak tree at the bend in the path, looking at the sky. At ground level, the branches were rustling in a faint breeze. High above, the clouds were dancing in the light of the full moon, driven by squall after squall from west to east. Back in my room again, sitting perched on the windowsill with my feet dangling above the porch roof, I could not tear my eyes away from the wind-blown clouds. The moon appeared and disappeared. Whenever it was veiled, the night became incandescent.

During the common prayer this morning, the conviction came that no burden would be too great. Everything seemed desirable. And now the day continues, bathed in that peaceful light, with the certainty of a presence.

Why are such moments of intensity so easily forgotten, as though they had never been? It is not a waste of time to note them down.

August 8, 1973

There are people who always want to be in at the start. If they have not been involved in the initial stages of a creation, they do not care to be associated with it. Do they not understand that there is no more creativity present at the beginnings of a venture than later on? Creativity is sometimes expressed more in continuity and duration. Otherwise all that remains is the short-lived adventure, but when the dazzling fireworks have burned out, we are left in the dark.

For us here at Taizé, creativity is as manifest in the last twelve years as it was in the first ones.

October 23, 1973

Birthday lunch for one of my brothers. We invited Cristobal. We talk about the flooding in southern Spain. Cristobal recalls how, when he was ten, he saw a river burst its banks and a torrent of water and mud come crashing down. Before his very eyes, the house of his best friend, Eduardo, was destroyed. As the walls collapsed he saw Eduardo's body being swept away by the waters. During the whole of the next week, every day he spent time in the local church, before the Sacrament. He wrestled with God, asking why Eduardo was gone. After eight days he found peace. He had told God, "You are all I have."

At that point, Cristobal began to cry; he wept for a long, long time. We decided to leave the dessert for another time and Cristobal promised, "I will come and sing flamencos." At table tonight, tirelessly, Cristobal sang.

October 24, 1973

Gather everything that happens, trivialities included, without reservation, regret, or nostalgia, in inexhaustible wonder.

Set out, forward, one step at a time, from doubt toward faith, not worrying about the impossible ahead. Light fire, even with the thorns that tear you.

December 4, 1973

For the last few days nothing more could be done for my mother; she could no longer take nourishment. This morning she was eager to calm everyone, and to one of my brothers she said, "Life is beautiful," adding, "We should always be glad." This afternoon she murmured once more, "Life is beautiful," then repeated several times, "Jésus...c'est beau." Those were her last words. At eight this evening, while we were in church for the common prayer, she entered Christ's eternity. She passed away gently, her breath simply slowing to a halt.

A few years ago, after her first heart attack, as soon as she could speak again she uttered these words, "I have no fear of dying, I know in whom I believe...but I love life."

September 4, 1974

When I was young, at a time when Europe was torn apart by so many conflicts, I kept on asking myself: Why all these confrontations? Why do so many people, even Christians, condemn one another out of hand? And I wondered: is there, on this earth, a way of reaching complete understanding of others? Then came a day — I can still remember the date, and I could describe the place: the subdued light of a late summer evening, darkness settling over the countryside — a day when I made a decision. I said to myself, if this way does exist, begin with yourself and resolve to understand every person fully. That day, I was certain the vow I had made was for life. It involved nothing less than returning again and again, my whole life long, to this irrevocable decision: seek to understand all, rather than to be understood.

— *The Wonder of a Love* *

September 10, 1974

I remarked last night to Hassan: your presence here guarantees that soon we shall be unable to speak of the love of God without discovering the treasures of trust in him found in the tradition of your fathers, Islam.

April 26, 1975

A mild night. In the distance, through the white mist lit by the full moon, the outlines of the hills of Cortambert and Bray are visible. Happiness: there it is, within reach. Never seek it, it would only flee. It lies in attentiveness and in wonder. Happiness seems sometimes to disappear for a long, long time.

And yet there it is, when eyes meet. There it is, close at hand, when a man loves, without really knowing if he is loved in return. And if, as well, this man can feel that many love him, then he ought to be filled with a happiness beyond words....

September 20, 1975

One day St. Teresa of Avila and St. John of the Cross met for a meal. Grapes were brought in. "I'm not going to eat any," said John of the Cross. "Too many people have none."

---

*Journal entries from September 1974 through June 1976 are taken from *The Wonder of a Love.*

Teresa answered, "I, on the contrary, am going to eat them, to praise God for these grapes." Their conversation mirrors one of the tensions of the contemporary Church.

January 3, 1976

Commit everything to him, with the heart of a child. Abandon yourself to him. Entrust to him all that goes against your heart or upsets your plans; pray for your opponent. And sometimes even go so far as to cry out your pain, when trials abound. Dare to use blunt, strong language: he understands it, even if others cannot. Entrust to him now and always whatever disturbs and torments you. And, keep silence in his presence.

Then, little by little, the praise of his love becomes the only thing that matters. Play within me, organs and zithers. Flutes, sing in me. Soft sounds and jubilant music, all together: let nothing stop the indispensable praise of his love.

March 25, 1976

A young man asks me how to face the dryness, sometimes the emptiness, of his prayer. When, in their heart of hearts, a someone knows that they are loved forever and ever, they are not afraid to wait in silence, even if some silences were to last until death.

June 4, 1976

A few moments in the pottery. On a blackboard where the young brothers who work there are in the habit of writing a quotation, there are these words: "Your love, O Christ, has wounded my soul; I go forward singing your praises."

Are they the authors of such a profound thought? No, it was written in the seventh century by John Climacus in his old age. At the age of fifteen, he had entered the monastery of Sinai. He realized that a passion for Christ is expressed through a person's whole being, flesh and spirit.

May 24, 1977

Some of my young brothers are passionately interested in the Scriptures. This afternoon, a few of us were talking about some almost incomprehensible Gospel sayings. How to make them understandable to young people? Those words cannot be taken in isolation. The Gospel can only be considered as a whole. Just as each of us wishes to be appreciated in the context of our whole life, and not in one isolated situation, in the same way it is important to see the words of the Bible in the context of Scripture as a whole.

Very often, we approach Scripture as if we were reading a letter from someone we love above all else, but who is writing to us in an unknown tongue. We try to translate at least a few words, the simplest ones if possible. What remains inaccessible in the Gospel, we can just leave alone. Later on, others will help us to understand.

— And Your Deserts Shall Flower *

May 31, 1977

A "parable of community" can be recognized when it speaks for itself and can be understood without any explanations. When I was very young, I was deeply aware of this at a time when I was confronted with this alternative: either to be a

---

*Journal entries from May 1977 through October 1978 are taken from *And Your Deserts Shall Flower.*

writer (while living in the country), expressing myself primarily with my pen; or else foster the creation of a "parable of community." In the end, the decision came of its own accord. May this parable be able to speak for itself!

August 31, 1977

I repeated to a girl from Belgium who spoke of her deep unhappiness: anyone who looks only at themselves will inevitably sink into melancholy. Open your eyes to creation all around you, and the shadows already begin to disperse.

April 22, 1978

Very often a man or a woman who dared to pray alone in a church has been, by their perseverance, a living appeal to others. It only takes one for many to be drawn along in the end.

August 7, 1978

For whoever has learned to love, for whoever has learned to suffer, life is imbued with serene beauty.

October 22, 1978

When I arrived this afternoon in front of John Paul II, I said to him: "Praised be Jesus Christ for giving us such a good Pope!" He answered: "Brother Roger, come and see me often!" After speaking to all the delegations which had come to Rome for the beginning of his ministry, he addressed me again: "Before separating we are all going to hold hands as a sign that we want reconciliation. We do want reconciliation, don't we, Brother Roger?"

June 4, 1979

Beside me a little girl of nine, her eyes wet with tears of distress. She has to leave us today. She loves coming to prayer three times a day. She is undergoing in her life the painful trial of human abandonment, that trauma of our time.

I write down for her: "Never forget that God loved you first. He has such confidence in you." Perhaps her grandmother will explain these words and adapt them to her years. Perhaps she will understand them all by herself prematurely, since so much maturity is already visible in her.

— *A Heart That Trusts* *

June 12, 1979

Abraham sets out in trust, not knowing where he is going. He has this adventure: he is asked to prepare a burnt-offering, his son Isaac. His son says to him: "Here is the wood, here is the fire, but where is the lamb for the sacrifice?"

There is no journeying in faith without having this question put to us, at least once in a lifetime, and without having to find out for ourselves what it is we are being asked to offer. But why be afraid of the will of God? It is love, and nothing else. God does not desire human suffering. The wood for this fire is whole-hearted trust. With that alone can the fire of a love be kindled.

---

*Journal entries from June 1979 through January 1981 are taken from *A Heart That Trusts*.

November 10, 1979

One of my brothers has written a note to help along the reflection to be undertaken among the native Americans in Chile. He points out how essential it is to call the Church to joyfulness, to sing still more, to discover all that fills her to overflowing at a time when so many Christians emphasize what is lacking.

May 2, 1980

In our church we have a copy of a seventh-century Coptic icon from Egypt. It shows Christ with his arm round the shoulder of an unknown friend. By this gesture he takes upon himself the burdens, the mistakes, all the loads pressing down upon the other.

Christ is not shown facing his friend; he walks along beside him, accompanying him. That unknown friend is each one of us.

January 4, 1981

A brother brings into my room a reproduction of one of the most ancient pictures in the catacombs: a man praying with both hands raised. This gesture comes down to us from the dawn of time, from humankind's first beginnings. A symbol of expectant waiting. Looking at it, I tell myself: like every Christian, you are first and foremost a man who waits expectantly, and prayer is one of the clearest symbols of this.

January 29, 1981

The foundation of our life is to know that God loves us. Everything in our existence springs up from that love.

May 10, 1971

I gave *Ta fête soit sans fin* [Festival] to be printed. Of all the pages written day after day in the last two years, which to choose? With the final period comes the question, Have I managed to say what I intended? No. Then why write? A boundary always remains, beyond which we are left alone with ourselves, whether we are writing or speaking spontaneously. — *Struggle and Contemplation*

7

Prayers

Christ Jesus, inner Light, do not let my darkness speak to me; make me able to welcome your love.

— *A Prospect of Happiness 2001* (Letter, 2001), 22

Holy Spirit, your presence is offered to everyone, and in you we find the consolation with which you can flood our lives. And we sense that, in prayer, we can entrust everything to you.

— *Peace of Heart in All Things*, 70

Jesus our joy, when we realize that you love us, something in us is soothed and even transformed. We ask you: what do you want from me? And by the Holy Spirit you reply: let nothing trouble you, I am praying in you, dare to give your life.

— *Prayer for Each Day*, 144

A thirst fills my soul, to surrender everything to you, Christ.

— *A Prospect of Happiness 2001* (Letter, 2001), 22

Living God, you bury our past in the heart of Christ and are going to take care of our future.

— *Prayer for Each Day*, 57

Christ Jesus, you did not come to earth to condemn the world but so that through you, the Risen Lord, every human being might find a path of communion (Jn 13:17). And when love goes to the point of forgiving, the heart, even when beset by trials, begins to live anew.

— Peace of Heart in All Things, 48

Holy Spirit, do not let our hearts be troubled, reassure us in our night, grant us your joy.

— Peace of Heart in All Things, 123

Searching for you, Christ, means discovering your presence even in the lonely places deep within us (Jn 14:18–20). Happy those who surrender themselves to you (Mt 11:28). Happy those who approach you with trusting hearts.

— Peace of Heart in All Things, 51

Holy Spirit, Comforter, in a world where we can be disconcerted by the suffering of the innocent, enable us to be for them a reflection of your compassion.

— God Is Love Alone, 49

In all things peace of heart, joy, simplicity, and mercy.

— Prayer for Each Day, 10

Words of Pope John Paul II at Taizé

Pope John Paul II visited the Taizé community on October 5, 1986. During the prayer together, the pope explained the meaning of his visit to the young people present:

One passes through Taizé as one passes close to a spring of water. The traveler stops, quenches his thirst, and continues on his way. The brothers of the community, you know, do not want to keep you. They want, in prayer and silence, to enable you to drink the living water promised by Christ, to know his joy, to discern his presence, to respond to his call, then to set out again to witness to his love and to serve your brothers and sisters in your parishes, your schools, your universities, and in all your places of work.

Today in all the churches and Christian communities, and even among the highest political leaders in the world, the Taizé community is known for the trust always full of hope that it places in the young. It is above all because I share this trust and this hope that I have come here this morning.

After the prayer, John Paul II met with the brothers of the community:

Dear Brothers, in the family-like intimacy of this brief meeting, I would like to express to you my affection and my trust with these simple words with which Pope John XXIII, who loved you so much, greeted Brother Roger one day: "Ah, Taizé, that little springtime!"

My desire is that the Lord may keep you like a springtime that blossoms and that he keep you little, in the joy of the Gospel and the transparency of brotherly love.

Each of you came here to live in the mercy of God and the community of his brothers. In consecrating your whole being to Christ for love of him, you have found both of these.

But in addition, although you did not look for it, you have seen young people from everywhere come to you by the thousands, attracted by your prayer and your community life. How can we not think that these young people are the gift and the means that the Lord gives you to stimulate you to remain together, in the joy and the freshness of your gift, as a springtime for all who are searching for true life?

Throughout your days, work, rest, prayer, everything is enlivened by the Word of God that takes hold of you, that keeps you little, in other words children of the heavenly Father, brothers and servants of all in the joy of the Beatitudes.

I do not forget that in its unique, original, and in a certain sense provisional vocation, your community can awaken astonishment and encounter incomprehension and suspicion. But because of your passion for the reconciliation of all Christians in a full communion, because of your love for the Church, you will be able to continue, I am sure, to be open to the will of the Lord.

By listening to the criticisms or suggestions of Christians of different churches and Christian communities and keeping what is good, by remaining in dialogue with all but not hesitating to express your expectations and your projects, you will not disappoint the young, and you will be instrumental in making sure that the effort desired by Christ to recover the visible unity of his Body in the full communion of one same faith never slackens.

You know how much I personally consider ecumenism a necessity incumbent upon me, a pastoral priority in my ministry for which I count on your prayer.

By desiring to be yourselves a "parable of community," you will help all whom you meet to be faithful to their denominational ties, the fruit of their education and their choice in conscience, but also to enter more and more deeply into the mystery of communion that the Church is in God's plan.

By his gift to his Church, Christ liberates in every Christian forces of love and gives them a universal heart to be creators of justice and peace, able to unite to their contemplation a struggle along the lines of the Gospel for the integral liberation of human beings, of every human being and of the entire human being.

Dear Brothers, I thank you for having invited me and thus having given me the opportunity to return to Taizé. May the Lord bless you and keep you in his peace and his love!

— *The Sources of Taizé*, 82–84

Epilogue

The following is a very small selection from some of the words spoken and messages received at the time of Brother Roger's death.

...In the face of violence, we can respond only by peace. Brother Roger never stopped insisting on this. Peace requires a commitment of our whole being, inwardly and outwardly. It demands our whole person. So this evening, let us communicate peace to one another, and do everything we can so that each person stays in hope....

— FROM A MEDITATION LED IN THE CHURCH AT TAIZÉ
A FEW HOURS AFTER BROTHER ROGER'S DEATH

•

This morning I received very sad, tragic news.

During vespers yesterday afternoon, our beloved Brother Roger Schutz, founder of the Taizé community, was stabbed and killed, probably by a mentally disturbed woman.

This news has affected me even more because just yesterday I received a very moving, affectionate letter from Brother Roger. In it he wrote that from the depth of his heart he wanted to tell me that "we are in communion with you and with those who are gathered in Cologne [for the World Youth Days]."

Then he wrote that, because of his state of health, unfortunately he would not be able to come to Cologne in person, but that he would be present spiritually with his brothers.

At the end, he wrote in this letter that he hoped to come as soon as possible to Rome to meet with me and to tell me that "our community of Taizé wants to go forward in communion with the Holy Father." Then he wrote by hand: "Holy Father, I assure you of my sentiments of profound communion. Frère Roger of Taizé."

At this moment of sadness, we can only commend to the Lord's goodness the soul of this faithful servant of his. We know that from sadness... joy will be reborn.

Brother Roger is in the hands of eternal goodness, of eternal love; he has attained eternal joy. He invites and exhorts us to be faithful laborers in the Lord's vineyard, even in sad situations, certain that the Lord accompanies us and gives us his joy.   — POPE BENEDICT XVI

•

Brother Roger opened a road and led us on that road with exceptional energy and courage. Some intimate convictions led him to go forward tirelessly on that road. Allow me to mention just two of these convictions.

Often Brother Roger repeated these words: "God is united to every human being without exception." This confidence carried and will carry the ecumenical vocation of our little community. With the whole Church we want to believe this reality and to do everything to express it with our life. Brother Roger had all human beings in his heart, from every nation, in particular young people and children. We want to continue in his steps.

And the other conviction: Brother Roger constantly returned to that Gospel value which is kind-heartedness. It is not an empty word, but a force able to transform the world, because, through it, God is at work. In the face of evil, kind-heartedness is a vulnerable reality. But the life which Brother

Roger gave is a pledge that God's peace will have the last word for each person on our earth.

Since Brother Roger did not want many words to be spoken in churches, I would like to conclude by praying:

God of goodness, we entrust to your forgiveness Luminita Solcan who, in an act of sickness, put an end to the life of Brother Roger. With Christ on the cross we say to you: Father, forgive her, she does not know what she did.

Holy Spirit, we pray for the people of Romania and for the young Romanians whom we love so much in Taizé.

Christ of compassion, you enable us to be in communion with those who have gone before us, and who can remain so close to us. We entrust into your hands our brother Roger. Already he is contemplating the invisible. In his steps, you prepare us to welcome a ray of your brightness.

— Br. Alois, successor of Br. Roger
as prior of Taizé, at his funeral

•

My name is Meret and I am ten and a half years old. Last autumn I spent five days in Taizé during my vacation. My family and I came to the church every evening. I was so enthusiastic about Brother Roger, because he shone so much. With love! But now, when I heard that he lost his life in such a brutal way, I was very sad. — Meret, Switzerland

•

In these hours of deep turmoil, I felt that I absolutely had to write to you to express my compassion. Yesterday morning I learned of the violent, unexpected death of Brother Roger. Certainly I know him no better than all the other young people who have been lucky enough to visit Taizé, yet the news of his death has touched me deeply. After all, I owe him a huge amount.

It was three years ago, when I was fifteen, that I had the good fortune to go to Taizé for the first time. I've been back twice since. During those three visits, thanks to the singing, the quiet, peaceful atmosphere, I discovered God, the Love he bears us, his capacity to forgive us tirelessly. I have finally learned to live in peace with myself and with God. Without Taizé, I don't know if I would have encountered this God, almighty in Love, who matters so much to me today.

So I want to give thanks to God for Brother Roger and the work he undertook. Despite the brutal way he died, I find a consolation in my conviction that up there a place had been prepared for him equal to all the good he was able to do here.   — MATTHIEU, FRANCE

•

It was with deep pain that I learned of the tragic death of the founder of the community of Taizé, Brother Roger, whose earthly journey has been an example of Christian living, consecrated to the service of the Lord....Man of inspired words, man of prayer, zealous worker in the fields of Christ, his untiring search to establish relationships of peace and love among Christians and his commitment to transmitting the Christian ideal to the youth of Europe earned him a universal respect. I am convinced that the tragic death of Brother Roger is an immense loss for the entire Christian world. I express my sincere condolences to all the members of the community of Taizé and I pray for the rest of Brother Roger, new inhabitant of heaven.

— ALEXIS, PATRIARCH OF MOSCOW AND OF ALL RUSSIA

•

Following the finest traditions of the faith that sustained him, Brother Roger consecrated his life to the service of peace, dialogue, and reconciliation. He became the untiring advocate of the values of respect, of tolerance, and of solidarity, in particular toward the young. His message of hope and trust will remain a source of inspiration for all. I am convinced that you will be able to pursue the work begun by Brother Roger. All my best wishes go with you in this exalting mission. — KOFI ANNAN, SECRETARY GENERAL OF THE UNITED NATIONS

•

Brother Roger lived so much with the Holy Spirit that his language possessed "a Gospel freshness." His words were so basic, so right, so simple, and so fruitful. They can live within us like the phrases of the Gospel, for what he said came from God. By his words Brother Roger enlightened my youth and helped me to understand Jesus better and to love his Church. Those words will probably live within me my whole life long. — CHRIS, USA

•

God has kept and will continue to keep the souls of the children, the brothers and all who witnessed what happened in Taizé. The concern for one another, the supernatural communion with one another was in all the pain and shock the strongest thing I have ever experienced in my life. It may sound absurd, but I am deeply thankful for what I have experienced, that I could be present in these most difficult hours of the community and experience the power of communion. I came alone to Taizé, but I did not feel alone for one second.... The prayers, the songs and the silence supported and comforted me more than ever before.

— HEIDEROSE, GERMANY

•

I express to you all my lively sympathy after the tragedy
that has robbed you of Brother Roger, radiant figure, peace-
maker, worker for reconciliation among all men. Incarnation
of tenderness toward all the creatures of God, he died of
that criminal violence that surrounds us. May his humanis-
tic ideals, to which he was so attached, endure thanks to the
faithfulness of his countless disciples. He had left his mark
on his age and shone forth far beyond his immediate field of
action.

— RICHARD WERTENSCHLAG, GRAND RABBI OF LYONS

•

There was a tremendous atmosphere of peace amid the mourning, at the funeral. In conversations with various members of
the extended Taizé family, I have come to feel that the martyr-
dom of Roger's death has somehow "sharpened" his message:
as if we received a short, sharp shock to make sure that we
had listened to his lifelong prophecy.   — JANE, UK

•

Many will talk about his gentleness, his wisdom, but beyond
all that I shall keep anchored inside of me his way of looking.
When I looked at him, I felt the happiness of those who have
made a choice, the happiness of his relationship with God,
the happiness of a beautiful, simple community life, the happiness of welcoming and opening wide the gates of Taizé. I
am part of the thousands of young people whose lives have
been deeply marked by Taizé and Brother Roger; there are
no words with which to express my gratitude.

— MARINE, BRITTANY, FRANCE

•

We have learned of the tragic passing away of Brother Roger.
Our hearts are full of sorrow as we stand with the Taizé community, near Cluny and worldwide, as well as those who are

mourning at this hour. At the same time we are very thankful for the extraordinary ministry accomplished by Brother Roger, particularly among young people.

— SETRI NYOMI, GENERAL SECRETARY,
WORLD ALLIANCE OF REFORMED CHURCHES

•

I send you my sincere condolences from the depths of my heart. Brother Roger was a righteous man among the righteous and a messenger of peace. That is how I knew him and that is how I will remember him. May the peace and the salvation of God be upon him!   — TAHAR, A MUSLIM

•

More than a guide or a spiritual master, Brother Roger was for many a kind of father, a reflection of the eternal Father and of the universality of his love.

— CARDINAL WALTER KASPER,
AT THE FUNERAL OF BR. ROGER

•

Even if I have never really seen Brother Roger, I dare say I knew him. You, all the brothers, were always speaking of him through the way you lived your daily lives. You bear the witness of Jesus Christ and of his beloved servant, Brother Roger. You have to keep going on this Way forever. You have to run forward, as the apostle Paul did. Never look back, but throw yourselves forward, tirelessly, and finally you will reach the end, in the hands of our Lord Jesus Christ.

— ANCA, ROMANIA

•

Dear brothers and friends,

Like all of you, I am still coming to terms with the terrible tragedy of last week.

But today is an occasion not only for mourning but for celebrating the extraordinary achievement of our dear

Brother Roger. Very few people in a generation manage to change the whole climate of a religious culture; but Brother Roger did just this. He changed the terms of reference for ecumenism by the challenge to Christians of diverse loyalties to live the monastic life together; he changed the image of Christianity itself for countless young people; he changed the churches' perception of the absolute priority of reconciliation, first in post-war Europe, then throughout the globe.

And what is perhaps most important is that he did this without any position of hierarchical authority, without any position within the politics and power struggles of the institution. His authority was authentically monastic — the authority of a father and elder brother in God who drew his vision from patient waiting on the Lord in prayer, and from the work and study and discernment of a committed community. His life and witness present the true Gospel challenge to all our Christian institutions, the challenge to become really credible through our willingness to live and listen in humility, to know where our true power lies.

We thank God today for a life that questions our institutional complacency, not in the name of fashion or ease or naive radicalism, but simply in the name of the Gospel of Jesus and the ministry of reconciliation. Brother Roger's life will be a lasting gift and challenge, and we pray that the community of Taizé, so much loved and valued in all the Christian world and beyond, will go on offering us this same gift in the years ahead.

Please be assured of the abiding love and prayers of your friends in the Anglican Church, and especially your brother in faith,   + ROWAN CANTUAR (ROWAN WILLIAMS),
ARCHBISHOP OF CANTERBURY

Bibliographical Note

Writings of Brother Roger of Taizé

Books

Communauté de Cluny: Notes explicatives. Lyons: Neveu, 1941.
Introduction à la vie communautaire. Geneva: Labor et Fides, 1944.
The Rule of Taizé. Les Presses de Taizé, 1961; New York: Seabury Press, 1968.
Unity: Man's Tomorrow. London: Faith Press, 1962.
Violent for Peace. Philadelphia: Westminster, 1970.
Living Today for God. London: Faith Press 1972; New York: Seabury Press, 1981.
The Dynamic of the Provisional. London: Mowbray, 1981.
Parable of Community. New York: Seabury Press, 1981.
No Greater Love: The Sources of Taizé. Collegeville, Minn.: Liturgical Press, 1991.
The Sources of Taizé. Chicago: GIA Publications, 2000.
God Is Love Alone. Chicago: GIA Publications, 2003.
Peace of Heart in All Things. Chicago: GIA Publications, 1996; new edition, 2004.

Journal

Festival. New York: Crossroad, 1973.
Struggle and Contemplation. New York: Crossroad, 1974.
A Life We Never Dared Hope For. New York: Seabury Press, 1981.
The Wonder of a Love. London: Mowbray, 1981.
And Your Deserts Shall Flower. London: Mowbray, 1984.
A Heart That Trusts. London: Mowbray, 1986.
His Love Is a Fire. London: Mowbray, 1990.

Books Written with Mother Teresa

Mary Mother of Reconciliation. Cleveland: Pilgrim Press, 1987.
Meditation on the Way of the Cross. Cleveland: Pilgrim Press, 1987.
Prayer: Seeking the Heart of God. London: HarperCollins, 1992.

Letters

All the following letters were published by Ateliers et Presses de Taizé.

Living beyond Every Hope (1974)
Letter to the People of God (1974)
Letter from Calcutta — Second Letter to the People of God (1976)
Letter to All Generations (1978)
Letter from Africa (1979)
Letter to All Communities (1980)
Letter from Italy (1981)
Letter from Warsaw (1982)
Letter from the Catacombs — A Call to the Churches (1983)
Letter from Haiti (1984)
Letter from the Desert (1985)
Letter from Madras (1986)
Living Springs — A Letter on the Inner Life (1987)
Letter from Ethiopia (1988)
Letter from Russia (1989)
Wellsprings of Trust (1990)
Letter from Prague (1991)
A Love, Source of Freedom (1992)
Awaken to a Joy (1993)
From One Beginning to Another (1994)
The Wonder of a Love (1995)
Choose to Love (1996)
From Doubt to the Brightness of a Communion (1997)
Joy Untold (1998)
Letter 1999–2001 (1999)

Astonished by Joy (2000)
A Prospect of Happiness? (2001)
Love and Say It with Your Life (2002)
A God Who Simply Loves (2003)
To the Sources of Joy (2004)
A Future of Peace (2005)

About Brother Roger and the Taizé Community

Clément, Olivier. *Taizé, a Meaning to Life.* Chicago: GIA Publications, 1997.

Gonzales-Balado, José Luis. *The Story of Taizé.* London: Mowbray, 1980; London: Continuum, 2003.

Opening Paths of Trust. Ateliers et Presses de Taizé, 2004.

Spink, Kathryn. *A Universal Heart: The Life and Vision of Brother Roger of Taizé.* London: SPCK; San Francisco: Harper & Row, 1986.

Taizé: Trust on Earth. Ateliers et Presses de Taizé, 1998.

Taizé Community. *Prayer for Each Day.* Chicago: GIA Publications, 1998.

Regularly updated information about the Taizé community and the meetings of young people is to be found in many languages on the Taizé Web site: *www.taize.fr.*